Conten

GW01184770

ISBN 0-9553628-0-6
978-0-9553628-0-4

Printed and bound in Ireland

Design, layout and photograph restoration by Suirvale Design & Print (052 42998).
Printed by Lion Print (062 61258)

Foreword

The history of the building of the canals and our inland navigations has been covered by a number of authors, most notably by Ruth Delaney. Gerard D'Arcy's *"Portrait of the Grand Canal"* gave us a great insight into the operational side of the Grand prior to its closure in 1960. More recently Joe O'Reilly and Caitriona Killaly's *"Through the Locks"* gave us an excellent first hand account of boatmen's memories of their time working on the canal.

This book has been compiled as a reference guide to the surviving trading boats that were used on Ireland's inland waterway system of rivers, lakes and canals. It documents the history of each known boat with technical and anecdotal information supported by photos from the past trading days to date. Many boats have been preserved by their evolvement to practical application and conversion over the years which has given a great diversity to the current fleet. A lot of the old photos, including some from the Shortall collection, have been digitally restored and preserved for future reference and are a magnificent photographic archive of times past.

Most of the barges featured have been out of working service longer than they were in it.

For example, 50M (the Venus) operated commercially with the Grand Canal Company for 32 years (1928 - 1960) but has been in private use with the Tottenham family for over 46 years. Likewise the 45M worked for 18 years (1928 – 1946) before it sank to the bottom of Lough Derg where it lay for 29 years (1946-1975) until it was raised by Donnachta Kennedy and authentically restored by David Coote. It has been cruising the waterways for the last 31 years as a constant reminder of our past industrial heritage. The Rambler hasn't been a work boat in almost 100 years and there are a good number of other boats still moving around our waterways that were built in the 19th century.

"As far as it is possible to befriend a piece of steel, I look on the 59M as an old friend who has repaid my efforts a hundred times over".

From the barge articles you will note that most have survived through three distinct stages, commonly referred to as their working life, their demise and their rejuvenation which reflect the transition from commercial to recreational service. The detailed mapping of this transition has become a core objective of this book together with the recording of the skippers and crew that served.

We trust that this publication will go some way to providing those that view these vessels with an appreciation for the historical contribution that both the barges and the crews made to our commercial development in times past.

As boat owners we are all proud of our boats and their history. Some owners are more passionate than others which is best summarised by the following statement, *"As far as it is possible to befriend a piece of steel, I look on the 59M as an old friend who has repaid my efforts a hundred times over"*.

I hope you enjoy the book.

Gerry Burke
Vice Chairman, Heritage Boat Association

Carrick-on-Shannon 2003

HBA boats Carlow 2005

Brendan Davis

HBA boats and members supporting the boatmen's reunion in Banagher 2006

Brendan Davis

The Grand Canal Company ...and the Bolinder Engine

The Grand Canal Company had long been aware of the problems of transportation on a mixed navigation of canal, river and lake. The existing fleet was mainly horse-drawn boats with a number of steam tugs which towed them across lakes and along the Shannon, with some attempts to tow trains of barges over long sections of canal. When internal combustion oil engines became available, the GCC bought a 4 cylinder Scott Sterling engine in 1910 which they installed in a barge in May, but it was not a success. The following year they purchased and installed four Bolinder engines. A trial trip was carried out in July 1911 and was reported to be "very satisfactory". More engines were ordered and by 1914 twentyeight former horse barges had been converted.

Prior to 1870 all boats, when registered, were given consecutive numbers. As the numbers had exceeded 1000 the company decided to start a new series, with the company's new boats being numbered, commencing with No. 1. Bye-traders (indepenent operators also known as hack boats) were started with 1B. The new series had not reached 100 when the suffix M (for motorised) was introduced to denote

"The starting ritual involves pre-heating the hot bulb with a blow-lamp and hand-pumping oil to the main bearings, big end, small end and piston, and greasing several exposed lesser bearings"

a company barge in which an engine had been installed. Company maintenance boats, usually older trade boats were given the suffix E to denote engineering. The government subsidised the building of twenty-nine horse-drawn barges during the second world war to cope with the transportations of turf to Dublin and these were denoted with the letter G.

The Bolinder Company

The Bolinder Company was founded in Stockholm, by the teenage brothers Karl and Jean Bolinder, in 1832. They first

The photo is of the next generation of Boatmen cooking their breakfast on the head of the Bolinder of 45M while it is being pre-heated before starting.

produced components for steam engines, railways and sawmill machinery but later developed their first internal combustion engine, a four-stroke hot bulb, in 1893. In 1903 E. A. Rundlof invented the two-stroke,

> *"Spontaneous loud explosions as the engine backfires contribute to spectator sport on the bank, followed by resolutions (over pints) to get rid of it and put in a proper engine"*

crank case scavenge hot bulb engine and passed it on to the Bolinders, who developed their range of semi-diesels from this—and the legend was born. The engines were so reliable and durable that they were used in barges throughout the world and Bolinder became synonymous with barge engine. The engines installed by the Grand Canal Company in 1911 were the 1908 E-type single-cylinder 8.35-litre direct reversing engines (invariably 15bhp). These were in continuous use in the fleet until CIE removed the last working Bolinder's from its maintenance boats in the mid-seventies. Consequently the E-type is known as the Irish engine. B boats eventually numbered up to 133B but a lot of these were former GCC boats that had been sold off. Most bye-traders followed the GCC lead and converted to engines.

How the engines work

The semi-diesel is the link between steam and internal combustion. A semi-diesel relies for combustion on heat and compression, whereas in Dr. Diesel's engine combustion is caused by compression alone. The vertical block of the Bolinder is surmounted by a pre-heated cast iron hollow hot bulb, where combustion takes place, driving down the piston through a vent in the bulb. This remains hot, allowing the fuel to combust and the air to change without high compression.

Peripherals such as the water-pump, fuel-oil pump and five lubricating-oil pumps in line, each with its own oil well, are driven by eccentrics from the shaft—all exposed and fully accessible in the steam engineering tradition. The silencer or expansion chamber is bolted to the block and is almost as large, being water-cooled by direct circulation with the engine. The starting ritual involves pre-heating the hot bulb with a blow-lamp and hand-pumping oil to the main bearings, big end, small end and piston, and greasing several exposed lesser bearings. Heating takes about ten minutes, but varies according to the age and condition of the bulb.

The Bolinder engine on 45M

Photo–Brendan Davis

At the crucial moment a few squirts of fuel are pumped into the bulb and a smart swing of the great flywheel, with the hand or the boot, results in compression and then combustion. Non-starting usually arises from attempting to start before the bulb is fully heated, with repeated squirts of fuel and exhaustive flywheel swinging—and an engine-room full of noxious diesel vapour. Spontaneous loud explosions as the engine backfires contribute to spectator sport on the bank, followed by resolutions (over pints) to get rid of it and put in a proper engine.

Overheating of the bulb causes expansion of the block and loss of compression, with the same result: non-starting and similar resolutions. Writing in 'Canal Mania' (Arum Press, 1993) Anthony Burton, the canal historian, deduced that life was seldom dull with a Bolinder!

The New Motor Fleet
The first thirty motor boats were all converted horse boats. In 1925 the Grand Canal Company ordered the building of a new fleet of custom-built steel motor canal-boats. The first one, 31M, was built by the Ringsend Dockyard Company at a cost of £1000. Between 1925 and 1939 forty-eight barges were built, most of them by the Ringsend Dockyard Company (known as McMillan's) and Vickers (Ireland) Ltd. (subsequently the Liffey Dockyard Company).

These boats were powered by the 15bhp E-type Bolinder and measured about 60' X 13' X 5' 6". They had bluff bows with accommodation forward for a crew of four. The cargo hold was 40', separated from the engine-room and bows by watertight bulkheads. The plates were quarter-inch and hot-riveted on angle frames. The barges were of rugged design and with the exception of the turn of the bilges, which are subject to constant wear, they have stood the test of time. Most of the new fleet are still around

and featured in this book.

A day at the harbour
Gerard D'Arcy, in his *Portrait of the Grand Canal* describes a typical day at the harbour in the early 1950s. The first sound at 5.00 or 6.00 was of a blow-lamp starting, followed by a colossal bang, back-firing, starting and further back-firing. (It was often difficult to get the bulb hot enough, with the old paraffin blow-lamps, to ensure a smooth start.)

After the engine was started, it was essential to keep the bulb hot, so the clutch was engaged as soon as possible and the throttle turned fully up. In the steam tradition there was no gearbox. The throttle was of the hit-and-miss variety peculiar to these engines. A striker on an eccentric engaged the end of the fuel-oil pump-piston, injecting some fuel into the bulb. The tension on a spring above the striker determined the frequency with which the striker engaged. At full tension and throttle, it engaged nearly every time. A short distance out from the harbour, dropping revs. and black smoke would indicate over-heating and pre-ignition. At this stage the engineer would introduce the combustion water, from a deck tank, in a gradual drip into the engine; this would cool the bulb, increasing the revs and ensuring a small puff of blue exhaust. The engine was now more or less set.

Locks
There was no reverse gear. To put the engine into reverse it was necessary to put it out of gear and then cut the engine, re-engaging it in reverse when it was just about to stall. The boatmen all exhibited great expertise at this procedure; however it was not something that was used routinely. With 47 tons of cargo and drawing 4' 6", the boats were run into the locks at high revs. and checked by an 80' rope whipped around the wooden stop post at the lock. The volume of water against the bluff bows

also acted as a brake. With the stop-rope made fast, the clutch was kept engaged at high revs. to keep the bulb hot and prevent the engine from cooling and stalling in the lock.

Then and now
So on to Shannon Harbour at about 4 mph, reaching Limerick in around four and a half days. But that was in the early 1950s and, while hot bulb handling was transformed subsequently by bottled propane/butane gas, in Ireland the Bolinder—with its unique sound—is going the way of the Corncrake.

At present there are only four boats—45M, 50M, 75M and 78M—that retain their original engines and all of them feature in this book.

In Britain, where canal heritage is cherished, the Bolinders are highly prized. Reconditioned and restored engines are frequently reinstalled in traditional narrowboats, attracting much attention at rallies, and Volvo (who acquired the Bolinder Company) present an annual trophy for the best-kept engine.

Misneach
Heritage Horse Boat No. 1

The Chairman of the Grand Canal Company, William Digges La Touche announced the order of two new iron trading boats on August 10th 1877. These boats were delivered in 1878 at a cost of £820. More iron boats were then ordered to take advantage of the then low cost of iron.

Horse drawn funeral, No. 1 Barge

The design and construction of the first two iron trading boats No.1 & No.2 was similar. A riveted structure with hatters felt between the joints. A characteristic of the iron 3/8inch cladding was the tendency to crack on heavy impact. Modern steel will bend and absorb an impact. A number of riveted patches were to be found on the hull, especially towards the stern. This was an indication of heavy use during its working life.

The earliest recorded weight for No.1 boat was at Killaloe Ballast office on the 30th of May 1900. Weights were added and the draft measured. At 48 tons she was down 4ft-6ins in the water. On board when weighed were 1 anchor chain, 4 covers, 5 ropes, 2 tiller handles, 3 skids, 10 rumors, 8 hatches, 3 trippers, 1 cork fender, 1 rope fender, 2 poles, and 1 boat hook.

While this boat is numbered No. 1 it wasn't the first boat on the Canal, but the start of a new numbering system and the first of a new fleet of iron boats purchased by the Grand Canal Company (GCC).

The boat had no engine but was drawn by

Misneach under reconstruction in Robertstown

a horse. Every bridge on the canal system carries evidence of the horse drawn tow line as it wore a groove into the limestone buttress. These boats carried wool, corn, wheat, beer, spirits and other goods with a

Misneach at Banagher

crew of 3 and 1 horse. Horses were changed and rested at various stations along the canal. Hazelhatch was the first such station from Dublin and the stables and associated buildings still exist today. With the introduction of the motor boats, No.1 was retired from trading service in 1928, but was retained for canal engineering uses. The sides of her were cut low to make shovelling the podelling clay easier from the boat. This is a clay with waterproof qualities, used to seal watertight the bottom and sides of the canal, thereby reducing the loss of water so essential for year round navigation of the system.

In the early sixty's Fr. P. J. Murphy (1935-1975) of Robertstown swapped an M Boat for the No.1 as it was being brought to James's St. Harbour for decommissioning. Fr. Murphy inspired the reawakening of interest in the Grand Canal and was involved in restoring a number of Canal Boats.

As a horse boat, No.1 then called "Pomeroy" held pride of place among the Robertstown fleet, being used on all special occasions. In the early sixties she carried a coffin to a funeral in Robertstown. On the sad and sudden death of Fr. Murphy, the Robertstown Canal Project lost impetus

and Pomeroy lay for years rotting away on the bank in Robertstown.

Eventually Pomeroy was sold as it badly needed extensive repairs. Much of the bow, stern and hull had to have the plating replaced. The conversion design and most of the work were done by the new owners and No.1 was renamed Misneach which is the Gaelic for "Courage".

In the early 80's the boat got its first engine installed. It was an Allis Chalmers 6 cylinder BUDA that previously saw service driving an air moving unit at a Roadstone gypsum mine in the 1950's. Also added was a 2 inch diameter stainless steel propeller shaft and 24 x 32 inch propeller which were liberated from the Clondalkin Paper Mill on its closure. These had been previously used to mix the pulp from which the paper was made.

The antique Oak and Scots Pine used for the interior of the boat saw previous incarnations in the old Jameson Distillery, Dublin. On a warm day, the spirits from the old oak casks are known to give off the vapours.

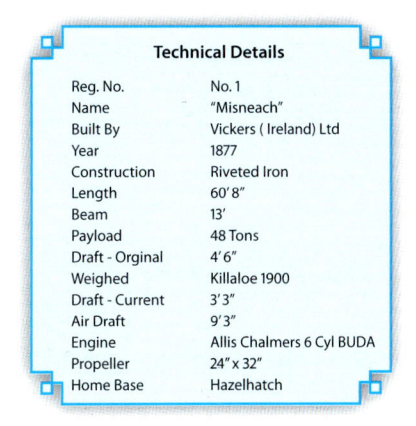

Technical Details	
Reg. No.	No. 1
Name	"Misneach"
Built By	Vickers (Ireland) Ltd
Year	1877
Construction	Riveted Iron
Length	60' 8"
Beam	13'
Payload	48 Tons
Draft - Orginal	4' 6"
Weighed	Killaloe 1900
Draft - Current	3' 3"
Air Draft	9' 3"
Engine	Allis Chalmers 6 Cyl BUDA
Propeller	24" x 32"
Home Base	Hazelhatch

Dabu
Heritage Horse Boat No. 2

Built in 1878, probably by Bewley & Webb, Dublin, who built most of the early iron trade boats, she would have cost in the region of £300. 61'3" in length and 13'3" wide, she is constructed of 3/8-inch Swedish iron, and her ribs, which are 2½" x 2½" angle iron, are at 2' centres. Everything is held together with "hot rivets" which are 2" apart.

Her pointed nose, rounded stern and her keel allow her to be moved easily through the water, as No.2 was designed as a horse boat and never had an engine in the trading days.

She was last weighed and calibrated in

The Bat (left) & Dabu (right) sunk in Killaloe c1960. Mick Donoghue in picture.

Killaloe in 1907, she would have carried all types of cargo, from manure, turf, coal and gravel to flour, wheat, Guinness and other general groceries.

No.2, as with all the other horse boats of the time, had a crew of 3, consisting of a captain, a deckhand and a horseman. The Captains quarters were at the stern of the boat and contained one bed and a closed fire. The crews quarters were at the bow and this room had 2 beds and a pot-bellied stove.

She ended her working days as a 'dumb barge' carrying muck and dirt etc. on the building of Ardnacrusha power station. Construction completed, she lay abandoned to a watery grave opposite the hotel in Killaloe. Seeing her sunk in Killaloe in 1966 Sean and Brigid Bayly fell in love with her design as No. 2 was unlike the other trade boats on the canal, which were flat nosed and flat bottomed. Raised from the bottom by John Weaving, she was towed up the canal to Clondalkin by Paddy Wilkinson on 76M, where her conversion to 12 berth cruiser would take place over the next 8 months.

A stern tube and No. 2's first engine, a Perkins 120hp S6M,

On the Barrow 2005

replaced by a more modern Ford 6 cylinder engine in 2004 and a new wheelhouse built in 2005. That combined with regular hull maintenance should ensure that she will still be seen around the system for many years to come. In 2005 she made the journey from Dublin to Waterford to partake in the Tall Ships festivities. 2006 will see her throughout the Shannon and Erne Navigations.

were installed between the 10th and 11th locks along with a timber superstructure and wheelhouse. After Sean's death in 1984, his son Robert (Robby) replaced the timber superstructure with a steel one and Dabu has continued to travel to all corners of our waterways ever since. The S6M was

On the Suir Estuary 2005

Technical Details	
Reg. No.	No. 2
Built	Bewley & Webb, Dublin
Year	1878
Construction	Riveted Swedish Iron
Length	60' 4"
Beam	13' 3"
Payload	50 Tons
Draft Loaded	4' 7"
Weighed	Killaloe 1907
Current Draft	3'
Engine	Horse drawn
	Perkins S6M
	Ford Diesel 120Hp
Home Base	Hazelhatch

Heritage Boat 31M

$31M$ was built in 1925 for the Grand Canal Company (GCC) by the Ringsend Dockyard Company for £1,100. It was the first boat of the new series of purpose built motorised (M) boats that the GCC were about to build so it was in effect a prototype boat. As with most prototypes it had its failings. Its main one being that it couldn't take a full load of porter in her hold. She had some other distinguishing characteristics, her bilges were unique in that they weren't rounded like other canal boats but were at an angle. It had portholes for the living quarters located in the front of the hull rather than the normal ones in the house.

Joe Connolly (Shannon Harbour) joined as greaser in July 1939. He went to replace Ned "Cutler" Connolly, at that time "Red" Mick Donoghue was Skipper, "Porter" Jack Farrell was deckman and Paddy Hoare was engineman. Paddy "Holy Joe" Donoghue also worked on 31M as deckman around that time. When "Red" Mick left, Paddy

31M Prior to going to Clondalkin

Hoare took charge and Jim "Twin" Moore from Athy joined as greaser. At another time Tom and Jimmy Doherty with Kieran Phelan worked on her. Other people that

Post rework at Landenstown

worked on her were "Devil" Connolly, Johnny McGrath, Paddy Reilly, Mick Kenny and Tom Doyle.

She was sold off to the Gills in Graiguenamagh at auction in 1960. They didn't do anything with her as her bilges were bad. In the 1970's they swapped 31M with a few pounds and got 78M, their fathers boat, in its place. A caravan was put in the hold of 31M and she was brought to Dublin in the early 1980's. At the time the OPW were doing a lot of work in Dublin. Tom and Bill Cox from Ticknevin and Tom Donavan from Pollagh lived in the caravan during the week. In 1988, Billy Flynn brought her back to Tullamore she lay unused until 1995.

In 1995, 31M was one of the canal boats

that were loaned out as community FAS projects and was given to the Clondalkin Community College for restoration. The work that took place included the complete replacement of the bottom of the boat including the replacements of the bilges (same as originally built) and the decks were cut back to around eight inches (originally 24"). The project came to an end prior to any conversion work taking place. Waterways Ireland got the boat back in 2003 and she is currently tied to the bank on the canal in Landenstown.

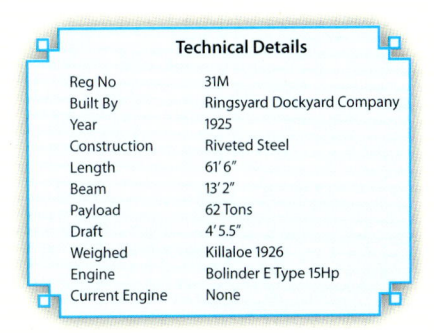

Technical Details

Reg No	31M
Built By	Ringsyard Dockyard Company
Year	1925
Construction	Riveted Steel
Length	61' 6"
Beam	13' 2"
Payload	62 Tons
Draft	4' 5.5"
Weighed	Killaloe 1926
Engine	Bolinder E Type 15Hp
Current Engine	None

John Merrigan loading malt

Whistler
Heritage Boat 34M

34M was built by the Ringsend Dockyard Company in 1927 and weighed in Killaloe on the 22nd of February 1928.

In the 1930's and the early 40's Paddy Pender (Prendergast) from Graiguenamagh as Skipper with his son Jack and his son-in-law John Hoar as the crew. Other crew at times were Jimmy "Mona" Bolger, Mick "Darkie" Bolger and Jimmy Grace worked on her as a Greaser. Around Easter 1947 Pat Hoar joined as Deckman, the crew then was John Hoar (his father) as Skipper, Jack Pender (his uncle) Engineman, by that time there were no greasers. When Jack Pender left sick, Robert "Bobsie" Mahon joined as engineman. Bosie later took out another boat and Jim "Scutch" Curran went engineman on 34M. In February 1949 Scutch left and Sean Hoar (brother of Pat) joined as Deckman

34M passes a working sailing ship

Courtesy — Shorthall Collection

34M in Shannon Harbour—May 2006

while Pat went engineman. Things were slowing down on the canal in Easter 1957 so Pat left to join the bus company in Dublin and Eamon Hoar another brother joined as engineman while Sean stayed as deckman. This was the last crew until the boat was left in when the canal closed down at Christmas 1959. Some of the cargos that were mentioned were bulk wheat, sugar and sugar beet, sundries. Butts, or large barrels, of Guinness were also a regular cargo for Corcoran's in Carlow for their bottling plant. One of the many unusual cargos mentioned was a load of cane sugar (brown sugar) loaded at Ringsend and taken to Carlow sugar factory to be refined.

34M was later sold off at auction by CIE. She was used by Martin Winston as a ferry craft to Illaunmore on Lough Derg for a number of years. Martin Winston sold her to David Coote around 1975. In 1976 David swapped 34M with Donnacha Kennedy for 45M. Donnacha had previously converted a number of boats known as "Weaver Boats" (40M, 42M & 47M) and converted 34M to similar specifications with felt roofs, and ship lapped superstructures. It is believed that she was used for a short while as a hire boat before selling her to Louis Smith. Louis used her on the Shannon as a pleasure boat for a while before selling her to Michael Hodgins who after a few years sold her around 1999 to her present owner. 34M currently lies in Shannon Harbour.

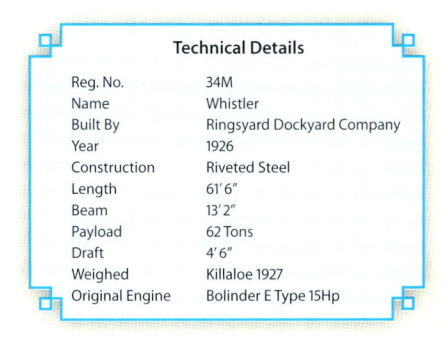

Technical Details	
Reg. No.	34M
Name	Whistler
Built By	Ringsyard Dockyard Company
Year	1926
Construction	Riveted Steel
Length	61' 6"
Beam	13' 2"
Payload	62 Tons
Draft	4' 6"
Weighed	Killaloe 1927
Original Engine	Bolinder E Type 15Hp

Courtesy — Shorthall Collection

34M in a lock

Heritage Boat 35M

35M was commissioned in March 1927 at Killaloe Co. Clare and her payload at the time was recorded at 61 tons. During the first phase of her life 35M carried cargo from Dublin down the Grand Canal and delivered along the way to the Shannon and down the Barrow. One sad note in 35M's history was that a young man named Roche, coincidently the same surname as the current skipper, drowned off her in Lowtown Lock. Not much is known about the incident other than he fell overboard when trying to load his bicycle onto her at night and was not discovered until the following morning.

When cargo deliveries by canal barge ceased 35M retired from that life in June 1960 and was converted to a dredger by the Office of Public Works. She worked away in that role until some time in the late 1960's when she was redecked and sold to Ballyteague GAA club in Co. Kildare. The club added a steel superstructure over the

On the Barrow—May 2005

original hold area and used her as their club bar for many years. She was sold on by Ballyteague Club in the late 1980's and rested on blocks in Verolme Dockyard in Cobh, Co. Cork from where her present owners, Andy and Cathy Roche, bought her in October 1992. They brought her by "trombone" low loader from Cork to the Shannon and subsequently to Shannon Harbour to start her current conversion.

Her "maiden voyage" with Cathy and Andy was in spring 1993 on the Grand Canal and was the first step in achieving the dream of converting her to a family holiday "home from home". Since then 35M has travelled much of the navigation, she made the trip from Lough Derg to Dublin with 68M, 4E and DABU to attend the launch of the Heritage Boat Association and World Canals Conference in 2001. During this trip 35M parted company with her wheelhouse. That incident was looked on as an opportunity

Courtesy — Shorthall Collection

to upgrade to the new one. That new one got some adjusting afterwards in Limerick but like all of the barges she proudly displays her war wounds.

35M has participated in several Boat Rallies on Lough Derg, on the Grand Canal and in Shannon Harbour with her present owners and their family. She visited Limerick in spring 2003 and travelled with a large fleet of other canal barges and heritage boats to the Shannon-Erne waterway and on to the end of navigation in Belleek in summer 2003. She travelled the Barrow to Carlow in the summer of 2005.

Like all of the old barges that worked the navigation 35M's heritage is so much interlinked with the men who worked on her. Pat Pender from Graiguenamanagh was 35M's first skipper after she was commissioned in 1927. Ned Pender was the next skipper with his cousin Dick as engine driver until 1947. Ned remained as skipper until then, the same year the locks in Shannon Harbour were extended and he then went to the larger St. Brigid. Paddy Hoare (Athy) was Greaser during the Greasers strike in 1936.

Tom Bowers took over as skipper from Ned with Jack Gaffney, a Kerryman known as "Sullivan" Gaffney, as engine driver and with Paddy Sullivan from Allenwood as deckman from 1948 to 1949. Paddy Sullivan was replaced by Joe Duggan as deckman for a short time and Jack Gaffney was replaced by a new engine driver, Butcher Cross – a Robertstown man and one of a number of the men who married in Killaloe. Other deckmen on 35M were Jackie Addley, Nanny Lyons and Paddy Nolan who worked on her for a short time from October 1955 to 1956. Bert Conroy, another man married in Killaloe, was later an engine driver and after him the engine man was Paddy Bagnall from Allenwood. Long Pat Pender, a brother of Ned Pender, took over as skipper from Tom Bowers and his son Tim was deckhand for a short time up to Christmas 1959.

The last skipper of 35M during her active service as a cargo vessel was Mick Conroy for the short period from Christmas 1959 until she retired from cargo service in June 1960, Simon "Hairy" Noonan (Robertstown/Killaloe) was Driver/ Engineman.

Technical Details		
Reg. No.	35M	
Built by	McMillans for Grand Canal Company	
Year	1926	
Length	61ft 6ins	
Beam	13ft 3ins	
Draft	1ft 6ins unladen, 4ft 6ins with full load, 3ft 3ins currently	
Payload	61 tons fully laden, 50 tons currently	
Weighed	Killaloe, Co. Clare 15 March 1927	
Engine	Originally fitted with a Bolinder. Current engine purchased from a fisheries boat in Killybegs and rebuilt in 1993 – Ford 120hp K Series 6 cylinder diesel.	
Steering	Original tiller replaced by hydraulic pump and ram system	
Home base	Cloondavaun Bay, Lough Derg	

Heritage Boat 36M

36M was built in 1927 at Ringsend Dockyard Company for the Grand Canal Company. Her Engine was a Bolinder like many others and she plied the Grand Canal and river Barrow due to her shallow draught. She was known by the boat men as a McMillan boat.

36M mainly carried, beet, sugar and fuel, but during her lifetime she did carry that special cargo "Guinness" which gave the M barges the nickname "The Guinness Barges".

In late 1960, 36M returned to Ringsend basin and because of the decline of canal transport she was retired and sunk off the quay wall just beside where U2 have their recording studio now.

In the early 70's Jimmy Dillon bought her and raised her. At some stage between her sinking and raising her original tiller arm went missing. 36M then spent some time at Harold's Cross, during that time there was a caravan in her hold. A few years later 36M was moved to Vicarstown where in 1981, Brendan Thompson bought her and began her restoration.

A new engine was installed, a 6 cylinder Ford D, and a superstructure was put over her hold. In 1984 she was moved under her own power to Shannon Harbour. Brendan along with many friends firstly removed over 20 ton of concrete, replated her bilges and replaced the original battered propeller.

Over the next 20 years 36M took shape, with Dave Whicher helping, Brendan and Dave spent many a long day working. Her interior is lined with maple and pitch pine, all doors in 36M are from old church confessional boxes, if only those doors could talk. The doors add to the charm of the interior as well as even heat distribution during the winter months due to the intricate carvings.

In 2000 Siobhán Hynes bought her from Brendan who put her up for sale, rather then let her go to someone else, Siobhán wanted to keep her in the Hynes/ Thompson family.

36M is home to Siobhán Hynes & John Thomson at Hazelhatch but she still travels the Grand

Courtesy — Shorthall Collection

Canal occasionally to attend the various rallies. Upkeep is continuous but then again she is over 79 years old and still puts many of the new boats to shame.

Crew Included—
Johnny Conroy who was the greaser in 1936 when the greasers went on strike. In November 1943 "Lamp" Conlon was in charge (Skipper) of her, Mick Tierney was driving, Tom Nolan was deckhand and Eddie Brennan was greaser.

36M in Vicarstown

When Eddy, left Paddy Nolan came on as greaser in his place. When "Lamp" left "Horse" Connolly went in charge. Later Martin Connolly (Shannon Harbour) went in charge of her and Tom Nolan his brother went driving. Mick Tiernan and Paddy Nolan gave up the Canal at that time. After a while Tom Nolan left her and Tommy Anderson came driving and Jim Nevin (Shannon Harbour) went as deckhand. In 1947 Paddy Connolly (Martin's brother) was in the St. James and he swapped onto

36M, Paddy went in charge and Martin stayed on as deckman. Paddy left the Canal around 1953 and went to America. Tommy Anderson also left at that time. Joe Mannion came in charge of her then and Paddy Farrell (brother of Peter), was with him. Joe Mannion left in 1957 and Tony O'Brien, (who survived the sinking of 45M) went in charge still with Paddy Farrell. Tod Kearney and Peter Boland also were supposed to have worked on 36M at one time or another.

36M in 2005

Caoife

Heritage Boat 39M

After the closure of the Grand Canal, in 1960, 39M was sold by auction to Ted Barrett of Lowtown. A syndicate of four led by David Coote subsequently bought her from Ted in 1964 and brought her to Dublin where she could be seen at Harcourt Terrace for

Courtesy — Shorthall Collection

many years. She spent some time on the North Shannon and in the late 70's returned to Lough Derg where she was used by various families over many weekends. 39M with David Coote was one of the 10 barges that went to Carrick-on-Shannon and on to Leitrim in 1972 to start with the opening of the Shannon-Erne waterway. In l986 it was bought by Bill Ahern. The barge was then extensively converted while lying at the 13th lock near Dublin. The timber superstructure was demolished. The barge was stripped back to the basic hull;

the decks were cut back 6 inches off each side to allow a greater span internally. The new superstructure was fitted in sections which was prefabricated in a factory and transported down to the 13th lock and welded in place. The original Bolinder engine was replaced by Perkins 6354 diesel engine from a Coca-Cola truck! A PRM hydraulic gear box, hydraulic steering, aqua drive and new shaft and propeller and cavitation plate were fitted. The Bolinder did not end up on the scrap heap, however as David Coote got it for spare parts for the 45M.

In order to have full head height from stern (wheelhouse) to bow, the layout was designed with tiered levels which results in an open plan design. The conversion took 3 years. Just when it was ready to leave the 13th Lock the canal banks burst near Edenderry so it was

During refit at the 13th lock

unable to travel to the Shannon. Two 50 ton cranes, one to lift the bow, and one to lift the stern were ordered. Both cranes nearly fell into the canal and failed to lift 39M. A 200 ton crane from Crane Hire finally lifted the barge. It was discovered that the barge weighed at this stage 54 tons and not 24 tons as estimated. After several attempts the barge was eventually loaded on to a low loader and left Sallins for Banagher. The low loader proceeded down the dual carriageway with the stern of the barge overhanging the trailer by 27 ft. After an adventurous trip through the country it was floated in Banagher.

39M is based in Coole Harbour near Garrykennedy and continues to enjoy life on Lough Derg, hopefully for many generations to come.

Crew Included—
Scotchman Connolly was her first skipper. Three men from Rhode–Joe Cox,

John Dunn and Con Lenihan were her crew for around 1948 to 1952-53. Jim Cox Ticknevin Christy "Ninthly" Bligh and his son Christy Bligh were on her after that. Dan McDermott, Tom Noon and Tom's son also spent some time on her.

Her last crew was John Coyne, Peter "Gurkyman" Anderson and his son Sean.

Technical Details	
Reg. No.	39M
Built By	Ringsend Dockyard Company
Year	1927
Construction	Riveted Steel
Length	61' 6"
Beam	13' 3"
Payload	60 Tons
Max Draft	4' 5.75"
Weighed	Killaloe 1928
Engine Original	Bolinder E Type 15Hp
	Perkins 6354 with PRM gearbox
Home Base	Coole Harbour, Garrykennedy

At Coole Harbour on Lough Derg

Sequoia
Heritage Boat 40M

40M With 54M & 74M

Built in 1927, in the Liffey Dockyard, by Vickers and weighed on 24th of February 1928 in Killaloe. She traded along the navigations carrying various goods for the Grand Canal Company but was also hired out as a Bye-Trader to a Patsy Goran for a couple of years in the early 1940's. She transferred to CIE with the nationalisation of the states transport companies in 1950.

40M was sold at auction to Myles Digby around 1960, complete with Bolinder engine and later sold on to Donnacha Kennedy in 1965-66. He replaced the original Bolinder engine with a three cylinder Ailsa Craig engine. Donnacha converted her and a number of boats for hire on the Shannon. These were called Weaver Boats, her accommodation consisted of 10 passenger berths with the skipper's berth in the engine room and the cook's in a corridor.

In 1976 Sean and Maeve Mathews bought "Sequioa" so named by Donnacha after a Californian Redwood Tree. In 1981 Jack and Aideen Roberts bought her from the Mathews. The day they purchased the boat coincided with the wedding of Joan O'Riordan and Joe McCool of the Snark (42B). Jack replaced the Ailsa Craig engine the following year with a Ford/Thornycroft. In 1984 a wheelhouse and heating system were added while moored in Edenderry. The bilges were re-plated in the early 1990's. While with Jack and Aideen, "Sequoia" was classed as the "luxury barge" on the Shannon, being an inspiration to all who were in the process of converting their own boats.

Aideen sold the boat to Jim Dillion around 1997. 40M was then moved from her old base in Terryglass to Shannon Harbour where she was based for some time. Her current

40M Running tied to 38M

Courtesy — Shorthall Collection

40M Working in Waterford Courtesy — Shorthall Collection

of theirs was another crew. In the latter 40's Jimmy Leason was in charge of her, Christy Blight was driving and Johnny McGrath was deck hand. The Canal was closed for almost a year in 1953/54 which resulted in some crews being let go. After the canal re-opened in 1954 Matt, Abie and Andy Maloney took her out. Matt and Abie left and went to England in 1955. After that Andy went in charge with Tick Donelan and Peter "Gib" Kenny. Kenny left and Paddy Nolan came in his place. Tucker Ennis was also in her for a while. She was left in for repairs around 1956 and after which Addy Danger and John Joe McDermott took her out. She was laid up in 1958 due to engine problems.

owner purchased her around 2000.

Crew Included—

Bill Melia was her first Skipper in 1928. Sam and Jim Cox from Banagher along with Dinny Weir crewed her for a while after that. Jack and Cristy Holt with a nephew

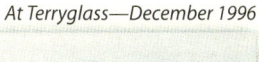

At Terryglass—December 1996

Heritage Boat 41M

41M was taken to Killaloe for weighing by her first skipper Jim Moore from Kildare in May 1927. From then on to the closure of the Grand Canal in 1959 she carried general cargo to all corners of the navigation. A number of events both sad and humorous are worth mentioning.

One tragic event happened on the 22nd of April (Easter Sunday) 1938 when Thomas Farrell age 19 from the Lock house in Tullamore was drowned when he slipped into the Canal off the decks of 41M. To this day, there is still a cross marking the spot at Rhode Bridge.

In 1957, 41M with Jack Nolan and Jim Farrell were returning to Dublin late at night with a load of 'empties'. 53M driven by Andy Maloney with a full load of porter was coming the other way, neither boat was carrying a lamp and just below Geoghans lock

41M with 60M

Courtesy — Shorthall Collection

(34th lock near Shannon Harbour) the two boats ran head on into each other. Luckily nobody was hurt, but the empties from

The 41M near Sallins around 1954

41M were thrown all over the place but the pointed bow of the 53M left her indelible mark to this day on the bow of the 41M. The usual singing while at the tiller was muted that night.

The 41M was the last barge into Carrick-on-Shannon in May 1959 carrying 20 tons of flour from Ranks in Limerick, and there is a plaque on the wall of the Old Barrel Store in Carrick commemorating this event.

When the Canal closed down in 1959 41M was left to die but fortunately was rescued by John Conway, who built her first superstructure using windows and pitch pine from an old factory. The pitch pine is still on her roof, but the windows have been upgraded to double glazed PVC. John later traded the 41M for an island in Lough Key one inebriated night. After that 41M went into decline again. Tim Kennedy purchased her, added a Leyland E170 6 cylinder Matilda tank engine, installed hand rails all round and repaired her bottom. Tim used her for a number of years, but left the inside very open.

In 1984, Les Saunders while cruising through Tullamore noticed the 41M looking sad and neglected in the inner harbour. A few months later he did a deal and bought her. Since then the engine and front cuddy have been replaced, the bottom has been replated and a large wheelhouse and double glazed windows fitted. She still boasts the original decks and propeller, and of course is proud to wear that special dent planted on her by the 53M in 1957.

Crew included—

During the 1930s the Skipper was George Duggan from Allenwood, and the crew were Joe Connolly from Shannon Harbour, Martin 'Hatpin' Doolin, and Christy Brien from Daingean. Tom Lyons was the engine man in 1938 when Thomas Farrell was drowned. In April 1941 Joe Connolly was back temporarily as deckman as Jim Connolly from Killina was out sick. At that time "Hatpin" was in charge, George Duggan was engineman and Nicky Conlon was greaser. Joe left a few months later when Jim came back. In the 1940s, Paddy Tierney took charge and was joined by Jack 'B&I' Dunne, Tony Hutchinson and Mick Clarke from Mayo. Mick eventually went in charge and stayed in charge until 1950, when he married B&I's daughter and emigrated to America. At the end of the 1940s, Pat McGrath was on 41M when she sank in the Ardnacrusha tailrace. They had a load of cement on board, but fortunately she was retrieved prior to the cement setting.

In 1950 Jack Brazil from Ballycommon went in charge with B&I as engine

Technical Details	
Reg. No.	41M
Built By	Vickers (Ireland) Ltd
Year	1927
Construction	Riveted Steel
Length	60'
Beam	13'
Payload	58 Tons
Max Draft	4' 5.5"
Weighed	Killaloe 1927
Engine Original	Bolinder E Type 15Hp
	Leyland E170 6 Cyl MatildaTank Engine
	Perkins 6354 with PRM 3:1 Gearbox
Home Base	Lough Derg

man, but later Jack swapped with Patsy Kennedy and Tom 'Nanny' Lyons who crewed the 41M until the breach in 1953. After the breach was repaired, Jack Nolan went in charge until Christmas 1959 when the 41M was decommissioned.

The last crew to handle the 41M were Jim Farrell, Jimmy Nolan (Jacks brother), Paddy Ruane and from 1958 John Coyne.

Other men connected with 41M were, Tom Connolly who worked on her in 1940, Tommy Nutt, Jim Leeson, Tom Doyle, Paddy Nolan and Tim Lenihan.

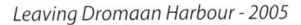
Leaving Dromaan Harbour - 2005

Heritage Boat 42M

42M was retired when the Canal ceased commercial operations in December 1959 and was sold off at auction by CIE in 1960. It was later bought by Donnacha Kennedy from Judge Connellan in Carnadoe in 1971. Donnacha converted the hull to a passenger charter boat and re-named her Jacaranda. The conversions were to similar specifications with felt roofs, and ship lapped superstructures. A small wheel house which had only three sides was mounted astern and access to the main cabin was by a stairway forward of the wheel house. The other boats in the fleet were 40M (Sequoia), 47M Palo Alto.

During the 1970's Jacaranda was chartered out to holiday makers for trips on the Shannon. They were provided with a skipper and a cook and mostly cruised the upper parts of the Shannon. In 1975 Jacaranda was used as the base of operations for raising the 45M from the bottom of Lough Derg. She was sold in 1977 to an Aer Lingus Pilot Charlie Coughlan who used her privately for the following ten years. In 1987 Stuart and Judy Hamilton bought her, built the current wheelhouse and re-fitted the interior. They sold her around 1996 to her current owner Cilian Fennell. Cilian has since replaced the engine and refitted the inside. She is known as 42M as he has dropped the name Jacaranda.

New Ross

Courtesy — Shorthall Collection

Crew included—

During a long and productive life as a commercial boat she was crewed by some very interesting characters including John Conroy whose son Jimmy is now the Lock keeper in Lowtown, Tommy Hannon, Paddy "Waxer" Dunne, Michael Connolly and Joe Cox.

Technical Details	
Reg. No.	42M
Built By	Vickers (Ireland) Ltd
Year	1928
Construction	Riveted Steel
Length	61' 6"
Beam	13' 2"
Payload	60 Tons
Draft	4' 5"
Weighed	Killaloe 1928
Engines	Bolinder E Type 15Hp
	3 Cylinder Ailsa Craig
	Ford 130hp 6 Cylinder Diesel
Home Base	Hazelhatch

42M at the 13th lock—2006

Courtesy — Shorthall Collection

Heritage Boat 43M

Like most Grand Canal Company boats 43M was used for carrying general cargo on the Grand Canal, River Shannon and River Barrow. 43M with her crew of Banagher Jack (Carroll) and Matt Maloney was the only other Canal Boat on Lough Derg on the first of Dec. 1946, the day that 45M sank. She was carrying a load of oats out of Ballinasloe for Kil laloe. As oats are a bulky cargo she could only carry about 43 tonnes of cargo which meant that she was riding higher out of the water than 45M. They had left Portumna early in the morning, hugged the Galway and Clare shore down the lake, tying up at the pier head in Killaloe before 45M made her fateful departure from Garrykennedy.

When the Canal closed down in 1960, 43M along with most of the fleet of boats was sold off at auction.

In Shannon Harbour—Note the cut down hull

In the 1960's Ted Barrett who operated a hire boat company on the Grand Canal bought 43M and made her into a dry dock by firstly cutting down her decks by 6". The operation involved bringing the barge into the lower chamber of the double lock at the 13th lock. The barge was then flooded and allowed to sink to the bottom of the lock. The boat requiring dry docking was

43M carrying a bulky cargo and "riding high"   Courtesy — Shorthall Collection

then floated in from the top chamber, over the sunken barge and the lock emptied so that the floating boat sat into the sunken barge. The barge hull was then pumped, raising the barge with the boat inside the hull which could then be taken back out of the lock and worked on. Removal from the barge was a reverse of that procedure.

In the early 1970's Gay Boylan bought 43M, fitted an engine and converted her to a house boat. She was involved in the building of George Spiers harbour in Terryglass during the 1970's and in 1985-86 she was part of the fleet that was responsible for the re-opening up of the Woodford river on Lough Derg.

43M was based in Garrykennedy for a good few years but has recently moved up to Leitrim.

Crew Included—
Around 1942 Paddy Reilly was in charge, Mick Kenny from Lowtown was deck man and Tom Doyle was engineman. Waxer Dunne, Scotsman Connolly, "Red" Willy and Paddy Connolly from Killina also worked on her at different times.

Technical Details

Reg. No.	43M
Built By	Vickers (Ireland) Ltd
Year	1928
Construction	Riveted Steel
Length	61'6"
Beam	13'3"
Payload	60 Tons
Max Draft	4'5.5"
Weighed	Killaloe 1928
Engine Original	Bolinder E Type 15Hp
Home Base	Leitrim

61M and 64M with a large boiler destined for the Athlone Woolen Mills

Sandpiper
Heritage Boat 44M

44M was built in 1928 by Vickers (Ireland) Ltd., as were all the 40 series of M barges. During her trading days she travelled extensively along the Barrow, Grand Canal and Shannon, carrying coal, malt, fertilizer, bricks, building material, maize, sand & gravel, hides, farmers & blacksmiths provisions and of course Porter. 44M had an extensive crew as she was a replacement boat when boats went in for repair. She had retired from service in 1957 due to leaking decks which were wetting the cargo of flour being carried at that time.

Like a number of Canal boats 44M has its own personal tragedies attached to it. In this case it was the drowning under the lock in Monasterevin, of a young lad in his teens, Christy Flood (Graiguenamagh) who worked on her as a Greaser. Her Skipper Jim Dunne was killed at Allenwood Cross when he left the boat for a brief visit home for a few hours.

In the 1960's 44M and 64M were sold to a man from Lough Neagh by the name of McFarland. Both barges were sailed up the

Top: On the banks of Lough Neagh–2005
Middle: Refloated
Bottom: Number revealed
Top & Middle picture show the missing sides

Courtesy — Shorthall Collection

Irish Sea to start a new life as sand barges. McFarland subsequently sold 44M to a Mr. Mullholland who drew sand with her for a number of years before finally abandoning her on the shores of Lough Neagh. She sank

and remained under water for a number of years before being re-floated in the 90's. Her luck wasn't great, as a short time later she was attacked with acetylene torches and most of the steel above water line was removed and stolen for scrap.

However her luck finally changed, when she was recently spotted, by a barge enthusiast, Michael Savage who identified the hull from the etching marks on the bow and set his mind on purchasing her with a view to restoration. Michael has since passed on the vision and the hull to Carson Grant and Helen Elliott who are about to embark on one of the most ambitious restoration projects ever taken on a modern M boat.

Crew included—

44M was first taken out by Jack Daly of Ticknevin. The Dohertys of Graiguenamanagh crewed her in and around 1944. James Maloney (Andy's father) and his sons Larry and Matt, Billy Carroll (Banagher Jack) were on 31M which was a small barge so they swapped to 44M with the Doherty's. Andy Maloney then came to her for the first time. The Sheridans, of Ballinaleague, along with Martin Carey (Ticknevin) also served on her when their boat 47M was in for repairs. Paddy and John Doherty and Paddy's son Paddy had her again in about 1950-51 before moving a few years later to 68M. Kit Farrell was then the skipper for a while as well as Jimmy Ruane of Rathangan. Dick and Bill Shorthall (Athy) worked with Jimmy at that time.

In 1954 Eamon Pender of Ticknevin and Jack Gaffney got 44M while their boat 61M was undergoing

repairs. An Allenwood crew consisting of Jim Dunne (Skipper), Pat Doyle had her in the mid 50's. When Jim Dunne was killed, Neddy Doyle of Allenwood took over and "Nanny" (Tom) Lyons went deckhand while Pat Doyle was in charge. After Nanny Lyons left, young John Doyle came to her leaving all Doyle's working together. Andy Maloney came in charge of her with "Tick (Tom) Donnellan, they spent a couple of months on her in 1957 before she finished up.

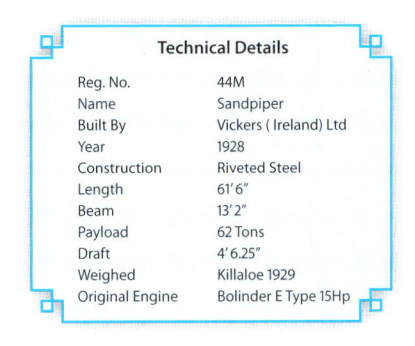

Technical Details	
Reg. No.	44M
Name	Sandpiper
Built By	Vickers (Ireland) Ltd
Year	1928
Construction	Riveted Steel
Length	61' 6"
Beam	13' 2"
Payload	62 Tons
Draft	4' 6.25"
Weighed	Killaloe 1929
Original Engine	Bolinder E Type 15Hp

Courtesy — Shorthall Collection

Heritage Boat 45M

45M was built in 1928 by Vickers(Ireland) Limited and worked for only 17 years before she sank in Lough Derg in December 1946 with the loss of three of her crew.

She operated as a Hack Boat, sub-leased by Tom Moore of Carlow, for about two years during the "Emergency", being used to carry sugar and general goods between Carlow and Dublin. She was also used for the shipment of turf into the city.

In November 1946 Christy "Copper" Cross was Skipper with Jack Boland driving and Tony Brien as deckhand. They had left Dublin with a cargo of porter for Limerick. "Copper's" father was seriously ill and on meeting 61M at Lowtown he swapped jobs with "Red" Ned Boland for the week so he would be close to home.

45M after being raised in 1976

Two days later on Sunday morning December 1st, 45M travelled down the lake from Portumna heading for Killaloe. The lake was fairly rough so they pulled into Kilgarvan. After a couple of hours they decided to chance going on to Killaloe so they headed off again. Two hours later they pulled into Garrykennedy for shelter. The St. James came down the lake afterwards and also called into Garrykennedy. In the late afternoon 45M lit the lamp (started the engine) and once again headed off down the lake. After a short while the St James followed her on, eventually taking the 45M under tow. Opposite Parkers Point 45M was struck by a gale that passed over the lake. The high winds caused the cargo to shift. The tow rope snapped as large waves swept across the deck and the barge heeled over and sank.

When she went down "Red" Ned Bolan, Jack Boland and Jimmy McGrath (who was Webbing) all died. Tony Brien swam to safety and was the only survivor.

Jack Boland's body was recovered the next day on the shore, "Red "Ned's body was found about three months later in Killaloe and Jimmy McGrath's remains were never recovered. "Copper's" father also died that fatal day.

45M lay at rest for the next 29 years at the bottom of Lough Derg. In 1975 after buying it from CIE for £20 Donnacha Kennedy salvaged 45M from where she rested in 80ft of water. 42M was used as a base of operations for the salvage, John Weaving and 125B and

Working before her sinking in 1946

when she carried a cargo of bricks, crystal and stout from Dublin to Limerick.

Crew included—

Her first skipper was Dan Logan. In January 1939 Joe Connolly, Shannon Harbour, joined the 45M as Greaser, at that time her crew were Mick "Oilhat" Connolly as skipper, Tom "Nanny" Lyons as deckman and Paddy "Smythy" Dunne as engineman. Tom Moore from Carlow with his two brothers Eddie and Jack, operated 45M as a Hack Boat.

a number of other boats were also involved in the operation which is a full story in itself. When she was brought up from the bottom the general condition of the hull was beyond their dreams as a thin crust of lime formed over everything and when that was knocked off the original paint showed underneath. To the everlasting credit of Swedish Engineering the Bolinder was started without a full dismantling or overhaul.

In 1976, David Coote bought 34M from Martin Winston with a view to restoring her to original working state. As Donnacha intended converting a hull and David restoring one, they agreed to swap and in March 1976 45M was sold to David Coote. She was moored at Hazelhatch for many years during her restoration, with the Bolinder being restored in the garage at home. Boat and engine were reunited in 1980 and she had her first voyage with her restored engine that year. In the mid 80's she travelled back to Lough Derg to her current moorings near Killaloe. She has travelled between Lough Derg and the Grand Canal in the years since then. 45M has been made famous world wide by the 1991 Waterways programme with Dick Warner, Dick and Declan Kearney

Technical Details	
Reg No	45M
Built By	Vickers (Ireland) Ltd
Year	1928
Construction	Riveted Steel
Length	61' 6"
Beam	13' 2"
Payload	62 Tons
Draft	4' 6"
Weighed	Killaloe 1928
Engine	Bolinder E Type 15Hp

On Lough Derg heading to Scarriff—August 2004

Palo Alto
Heritage Boat 47M

After a long and productive life as a commercial barge she was sold by CIE to the Dalkey Sea Scouts who had hoped to convert her to a clubhouse. However, this was not to come to pass, and after an idle year or two, she was bought by Donncha Kennedy in the 1960's, who installed a Ford 80HP six cylinder diesel engine internally cooled from water in the ballast tank. He also named her Palo Alto, teaming her up 40M- Sequoia, and 42M-Jacaranda as part of the charter fleet known as Weaver Boats. All these barges were to a similar specifications with felt roofs, and shiplapped superstructures. The original beams which were used to cover the hold, were used to support the roof, and the GCC stamp can still be seen on many of them today. A small wheel house which had only three sides was mounted astern and access to the main cabin was by a stairway forward of the wheel house. From the late 60's through the 70's and 80's Palo Alto was chartered, in many cases to Americans holidaying in Ireland. They were provided with a skipper and a cook and cruised the upper parts of the Shannon.

Palo Alto at liberty on the Liffey in 1997!

"Barges are funny looking boats—low, stubby and utilitarian"

The following description is an extract from the travel supplement to an American newspaper called "The Record" and dated 8th March 1987…"Barges are funny looking boats—low, stubby and utilitarian. The Palo Alto is no exception. Passengers are accommodated in four cabins, a bow cabin with two lower bunks, a large cabin with three quarter bed and two cabins rather like train compartments with upper and lower berths. There were two heads for use by passengers and crew, and a highly effective and comfortable shower. There were also two common rooms, a kitchen-dining room that was the centre of most activity, and a glass enclosed wheelhouse for viewing the panorama while staying dry."

The wheelhouse described above is not the

original. Donncha added this to the Palo Alto, after he had sold 40M and 42M in the 80's. The open stairwell was covered and access to below was through the wheel house. He also cut the tiller and fitted a chain driven, universal jointed, steering mechanism. The steering wheel itself is made of iron and was originally used on Kilmainham weir! Donncha never wasted anything!

In July 1990 while she was still being chartered, she was bought by her current owners Piaras and Pam O'Brien. They replaced the wheelhouse and made a few other changes down below. The engine was completely overhauled with a heat exchanger fitted to give her a wet exhaust. Since then they have travelled extensively to many parts of the Shannon and taken part in many rallies, including Shannon Harbour, North Shannon and Lough Derg. In 1997 she was taken to Dublin to take part in the annual Dublin Rally and managed to get as far as Capel St. Bridge on the Liffey. She is berthed in Gortmore Boat Club, and manages to travel as far as Lough Derg Yacht Club in Dromineer each summer, where she is used as a home away from home.

Crew Included—
Crews on the companies boats swapped and changed all the time, what we do know

Technical Details	
Reg. No.	47M
Built By	Vickers (Ireland) Ltd
Year	1928
Construction	Riveted Steel
Length	61' 6"
Beam	13' 2"
Payload	62 Tons
Max Draft	4' 6"
Weighed	Killaloe 1928
Engine	Bolinder E Type 15Hp
	Ford 80hp 6 Cyl Water Cooled
Steering	Chain Driven / Universal Jointed
Home Base	Gortmore Boat Club, Lough Derg

about 47M is that in the early 40's John "Pim" Donoghue was in charge (Skipper) with Tony Dunn driving (engineman), Larry Maloney was deckhand and Johnny Codd was greaser.

Around 1948 she was with the B arrow men for a while before being tied up. After that two guys called Bruton and Morin had her for one winter. The crew at one time were

In Shannon Harbour

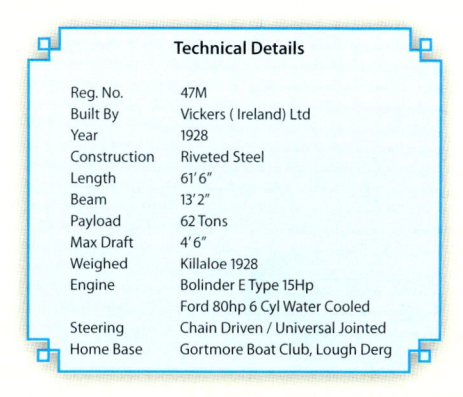

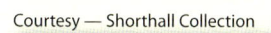
Courtesy — Shorthall Collection

Tony and Peter Brien and Peter (Peadar) Boland. At another time it was Paddy Day from Athy with Peter Boland and Paddy Addley. Her last Crew were Paddy McGrath with his two sons Larry and Paddy.

Cluaine Uaine Bheag
Heritage Boat 48M

48M was built by Vickers (Ireland) Ltd. in 1928 for the Grand Canal Company as a general motorised trade boat. She would have carried general cargo including Guinness to all parts of the navigation until the closure of the Grand

48M stranded on a breakwater block

Canal in 1959. She was subsequently sold off to the Malahide Dockyard as a general construction platform where she lay abandoned until she was found by George Spiers in the early 1967. George, along with Mick Rowan, acquired her where she lay precariously perched on a breakwater concrete block. They managed to float 48M on a high tide and have her towed by trawler

to the Liffey and up to James's Street Basin. Having concern for the condition of the hull it was exchanged for 93E which was sailed home. 48M remained in James's Street until it was transferred with the remaining barges to the Grand Canal in Ballycommon. These vessels were later moved into Tullamore Harbour for safety and she remained there until 1995 when she was selected to be one of the barges allocated to the FAS community project. 48M was leased to the Shannon Harbour Community Project and transferred by canal to the Dry Dock Shannon Harbour from which she was lifted by crane. Some delicate manoeuvring delivered her into the large Transhipping Shed which was the base for the full restoration. The restoration project ran from 1996 to 2003 converting her into a licensed passenger vessel to carry 50 passengers with 3 crew. Unfortunately the delivery of the complete barge ended the project and

Prior to restoration in Shannon Harbour

she was returned to Waterways Ireland and is currently stored in Tullamore Harbour.

48M with her new name

Crew included—
Paddy "Waxer" Dunne started on the Canal with his father on 48M in 1932.

Joe Cox from Tubberdaly was in charge in 1936, Tom Connolly from Forde Bridge was deckman and Jimmy "Buttermilk" Kelly from Tullamore was engineman.

Joe Connolly Shannon Harbour replaced Tony Dunne as a Greaser on September 20th 1937. In Feb 1938 "Buttermilk" left and Joe Cox's brother joined in his place. Jim Taylor, Johnny Press and Tom Cox also worked as deck men around this time after Tom Connolly moved on. Mick Coyne from Gillen also worked on her.

In the early 1940's "Joney" Judge was in charge for a while with Joe Connolly Shannon Harbour as driver and Tommy Nutt as deckman. Tom and Mick Donlon and Jimmy Reynolds all from Banagher along with Tom

Doyle worked on her at one time as did Jimmy Regan, Tom Flynn and Jim Gill

In February 1946 Joe Connolly (Shannon Harbour) returned as a driver joining his brother Paddy who was the Skipper. Jim Reynolds was deckman and Joe Manning was greaser. Reynolds left the following August and Joe Manning went as deckman. Billy Colton later replaced Joe Manning. In March 1947 Paddy left and Jim Nevin went in charge. Last working crew recorded in CIE records are John Dunne (Master) John Bracken (Engineman (Tpy)) and Conleth Lenihan (Deckman).

Technical Details

Reg. No.	48M
Built By	Vickers (Ireland) Ltd
Year	1928
Construction	Riveted Steel
Length	61' 6"
Beam	13' 2"
Payload	60 Tons
Draft	4' 5.5"
Weighed	Killaloe 1928
Engine	Bolinder E Type 15Hp
	Ford Mermaid Melody 2 4 Cyl. Diesel
Gearbox	Borg-Warner Gearbox
Generator	Ford Mermaid Melody II
Steering	Vetus Hydraulic

48M at Edenderry

Ye Iron Lung
Heritage Boat 49M

*A*t the end of her working life she was bought at auction in Shannon Harbour by the Anchor Hotel at Ballyleague (Lanesboro). Converted as a houseboat she provided living accommodation for workers constructing Rinenna (Shannon Airport).

The 49M returned to Lanesboro and was advertised for sale or rent. At this time she was painted white with light blue and was named the St. Mary. In the summer of 1961 Sean Fitzsimons hired the St. Mary for two weeks to do the Shannon boat rally. Following a great holiday Sean and John Connon decided to buy the barge between them for a figure believed to be £620.00.

They took possession of the barge on St. Stephens Day 1961 when it was delivered to Athlone and tied by one rope to the railings behind the library without fuel.

The plan at this stage was to bring the 49M to Dublin and work on her there, she was duly brought down to Shannon Harbour for the Dublin trip, but that winter was so severe the canal had frozen over. The barge eventually made St. James's Harbour in March of 1962. It is one of the very few barges ever to return to the now defunct Guinness Harbour after being sold into private hands. Sean and John felt that the harbour was not as safe as they had hoped for the renovations and moved back down the canal to the 12th lock where alterations were made to the lay out of the cabins and toilet. A pot bellied stove was also installed in the lounge. The chimney for this went through the superstructure of the top deck and was surrounded by a small barrel.

It was in the late 1950's and early 1960's that the now familiar aluminium kegs were replacing the old wooden beer barrels. These somehow got the nickname of iron lungs; also lung is the Irish name for ship and as the St. Mary was not considered a suitable name for the barge she was subsequently

Courtesy — Shorthall Collection

renamed "Ye Iron Lung".

The Iron Lung was then bought back down the canal and returned to the Shannon where she has been based in Athlone for more than 40 years. As well as all the Shannon boat rallies, the Lung has been found over the years at most rallies, work parties, hoolies and bun fights the length and breadth of the Shannon, the Grand Canal and was the first barge ever to navigate the Erne all the way to Belleek.

49M at Ballycommon in May 2006

Over the years various work has been done on the 'Lung'. When first bought she had an 'Atlantic' marine diesel engine fitted. Apparently the gearbox was so big that the engine was side mounted. This was later changed and a BMC 6-cylinder bus engine was installed, it is still this type of engine today but we believe it is probably on its second bus.

Sean once bought a second hand double decker and stripped out any parts he could for the barge. Aluminium panels were used for the side superstructure. The large windows were installed in the lounge, with the raised level of this and the amount of light allowed in there is a great feeling of space during the day, and plenty of room for a hooley at night. Also some of the bus seating was used for a time and could dou-ble for beds when the crew exceeded the twelve bunks she had up until very recently. The engine was taken out and used as previously mentioned. Sean then managed to sell the remaining windows and chassis

and still made a profit on the deal.

Having owned the barge for 40 years Sean found it was becoming too much without regular crew and decided to sell it in 2001. With his usual canniness he felt that by selling it to family he would have the best of both worlds, get rid of the responsibility but still enjoy use of the barge, hence he sold it to his nephew Andy Fitzsimons, the current owner.

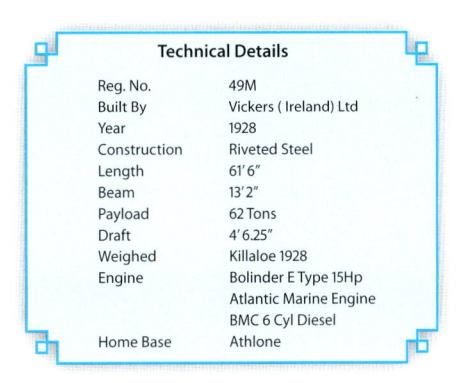

Technical Details

Reg. No.	49M
Built By	Vickers (Ireland) Ltd
Year	1928
Construction	Riveted Steel
Length	61' 6"
Beam	13' 2"
Payload	62 Tons
Draft	4' 6.25"
Weighed	Killaloe 1928
Engine	Bolinder E Type 15Hp
	Atlantic Marine Engine
	BMC 6 Cyl Diesel
Home Base	Athlone

The Venus
Heritage Boat 50M

The barge numbered 50M (formerly Grand Canal Company and CIE) was bought at the CIE auction on 8 June 1960 by Charles Tottenham, on behalf of himself and his brothers Robert, Geoffry and Richard. The price was £89.5s.0d. She was christened the Venus. They enlisted the help of Jimmy Dean, a former bargee, and brought her from the harbour at St James's Street to Williamstown, Co Clare, between 14-16 June and then to Scarriff dock. Dinny Weir, another former bargee, looked after her in Scarriff.

Jimmy Dean & Chuff (Springer Spaniel)—June 1960

Conversion started with 18 tones of hand-mixed concrete being poured into the hull for ballast. Over the next two years, the living accommodation was completed, often on the move. When it was complete, the Venus could sleep nine people and could take two cars on the roof. In 1971, Geoffry, his wife Ann Louise and his son John lived on the Venus while they were waiting for their house in Whitegate, Co Clare, to be renovated. During this time, the familiar marble busts were placed on the marks at Benjamin Rock and Horse Rock. The busts were of the owners' ancestors ("Lofty" and "Charlie") and were surplus to family requirements. They were put in place on a dark and foggy night departing from and returning to Scarriff.

In 1966, the Venus was probably the last boat to be hauled onto the slip at Killaloe, and almost didn't survive the experience. It took four people "from breakfast to lunch" to winch her onto dry land. While she was there, a fire broke out in the galley. By an odd stroke of luck, Davey Columbey, the head of the Killaloe fire service, was drinking tea on board at the time. He summoned his crew, led by J Kennedy, who quickly quelled the flames.

Visitors to the Venus are always struck by the collection of Guinness advertisements from the 1960s. Many feature the old animal prints with the slogans "Guinness for Strength" and "My Goodness, My Guinness". Most are still in place, though many have faded over time.

During a regatta in the 1960s, it is said that four barrels of Guinness were consumed on board the Venus. Without the proper taps, the Guinness was inclined to be "heady". This problem was overcome at the suggestion of Ken Simmons, who found that it settled nicely in a kettle or teapot before dispensing.

rtesy — Shorthall Collection

The Venus is one of the very few barges to have retained the old 15 HP Bolinder engine. This makes any journey quite a performance. To start the engine requires a blowlamp to be lit, and to start a large flywheel manually. The engine gives a very distinctive noise when moving, moves slowly and is very difficult to put into reverse.

Since the Venus was bought a log has been dutifully kept by the owners of all family holidays and fishing expeditions. Events in the log include the lifting out of the water in Kilgarvan of Dave Fogarty's tractor when it was driven by accident into the Shannon in 1961. In 1975 she assisted in the lifting of the 45M at Parkers Point. Unfortunately, less time has been spent on her in recent years, so that she is in need of serious renovation. It is hoped that this will be completed in the next 1-2 years.

Technical Details

Reg. No.	50M
Built By	Vickers (Ireland) Ltd
Year	1928
Construction	Riveted Steel
Length	61' 6"
Beam	13' 2"
Payload	62 Tons
Draft	4' 6"
Weighed	Killaloe 1928
Engine	Bolinder E Type 15Hp
Steering	Tiller
Home Base	Church Bay , Lough Derg

The Carpenter's Boat
Heritage Boat 51M

51M was built by Vickers in 1928. In 1930 there was a terrible accident when on a cold night the crew packed up the stove and went to bed. The night was so cold that they didn't have any port holes open so there was no ventilation. Two of the crew Dan Logan from Robertstown and Jack Grace from Blackwood died of

Courtesy — Shorthall Collection

suffocation during the night. The other two crew Peter Kelly from Ticknevin and Jim McDonnagh from Plucerstown were lucky to survive. In August 1945 Joe Connolly from Shannon Harbour joined the crew as deckman, at that time 'Guy' Bolger was skipper, Patsy Bill Bolger was engineman

On the Shannon after conversion

and Jim 'Pusheen' Bolger was greaser. Tom 'The Guy' Bolger also worked on her at one time. In 1960, 51M was the last boat out of

> *"She was used by the maintenance department —fixing locks etc.— and became known as the Carpenters boat"*

Dublin with a load of Guinness for Limerick. Tommy McCormack (Allenwood) was Skipper, Ned Doyle (Allenwood/Athy) was the Driver/Engineman.

Courtesy — Shorthall Collection

51M wasn't sold off in the 1960's with the rest of the boats but was retained by CIE. She was used by the maintenance department, fixing locks etc., and became known as the Carpenters boat. Ger O'Toole from Sallins was the Carpenter and Mick Convey from Rahan was his helper. At times Paddy Hannon also worked as a Carpenters helper. Ger and Mick were 51M's crew when the canal closed down in 1960 to mid 70's when Ger retired. After that she was converted by CIE in Tullamore into an accommodation boat for maintenance crews. She was also re-engined at that time. Following the conversion she was used on the Barrow and the Canal up to around 1989. Sometime later she moved to the Grand Canal Harbour in Ringsend where she still lies. 51M still belongs to Waterways Ireland.

Technical Details	
Reg. No.	51M
Built By	Vickers (Ireland) Ltd
Year	1928
Construction	Riveted Steel
Length	61' 6"
Beam	13' 2"
Payload	60 Tons
Draft	4' 5.5"
Weighed	Killaloe 1928
Engine	Bolinder E Type 15Hp
Steering	Tiller
Home Base	Ringsend

Courtesy — Shorthall Collection

The Eustace
Heritage Boat 52M

$52M$ was built for the Grand Canal Company in 1928 by Vickers in Dublin. Company boats had different crews on and off but we know that Michael and John Connolly from Graiguenamagh with Matt Duggan worked on her at one time. In February 1942 after the strike 52M was taken out by Paddy Connolly Shannon Harbour as skipper with his brother's, Tom as engineman, Joe as deckhand and Jim Nevin as greaser. Another crew were Mick McDonnagh with Bert Conroy and Tim Lehanin from Robertstown.

That crew had an unfortunate "directional incident" one morning leaving Killaloe with a load of porter for Limerick. On the return journey out of Limerick they had a load of Maize and 52M sank in the tailrace just below Parteen bridge. The story goes that she didn't sink immediately so the crew managed to get their bed clothes off and they slept on the bank for the night. The boat was left under water for the winter and was raised the following summer when water levels were lower.

The lock in Athy

After the Canal was closed in 1959, 52M was sold off by CIE to a Mr. A. Power who subsequently sold it on to Roadstone. Roadstone used her for a few years as a sand and gravel boat on the river Suir. In 1969 she was submerged in the river near Mooncoin and was in pretty bad shape when it was purchased by Robertstown Muintir na Tire for £350. That July she was towed to St. Mullins, by a pilot boat, for repairs. After repairs she was towed by 107B (another Robertstown Muintir na Tire boat) all the way back to Robertstown. In 1970 John Tyrell of Arklow designed a superstructure to accommodate 60 to 70 passengers. It took two years to do the converstion and when she was launched in 1972 by Mrs George Colley she was named the 'Eustace'. The name was in recognition of Colonel Charles Eustace one time Chairman of the court of directors of the Grand Canal. From then to 1980 the Eustace was used for passenger tours on the Grand Canal. In 1985 trips commenced again and she was used by RTE for a film 'The Stowaway' with a cast of children from Robertstown School.

The unique painted bow of the Eustace

In 1987 Dublin Eastern Regional Tourist Organisation (DERTO) was given possession of the boat and the hotel. Boat trips had ceased prior to this take-over so these were started up again. In 1990 Midlands Eastern

> *"The name was in recognition of Colonel Charles Eustace, one time Chairman of the court of directors of the Grand Canal"*

Regional Tourist Organisation (MERTO) took over the ownership and running of 52M, 107B and the hotel in Robertstown. The following year 52M got a new Ford 5000 engine. Two years later in 1992 Robertstown Community Development Association took a lease on the Eustace. The boat was refurbished and re-launched by Charlie McCreevy at the May Festival that year. She was once again back doing trips on the canal, it's got a bar aboard and was used for festivals, weddings, bus trips and school

tours. Sadly the level of business wasn't sufficient to keep the operation going so the "Eustace" is now back with MERTO awaiting a new lease of life.

Crew Included—

We know Michael and John Connolly from Graiguenamagh, with Matt Duggan, worked on her at one time. In February 1942 52M was taken out by Paddy Connolly Shannon Harbour as skipper with his brothers, Tom as engineman, Joe as deckhand and Jim Nevin as greaser. Another crew were Mick McDonnagh with Bert Conroy and Tim Lehanin from Robertstown.

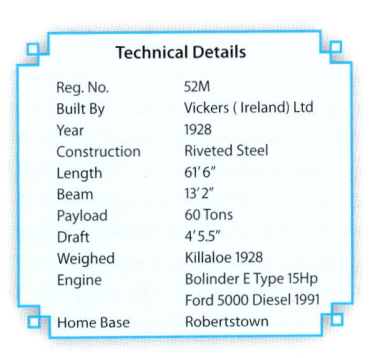

Technical Details	
Reg. No.	52M
Built By	Vickers (Ireland) Ltd
Year	1928
Construction	Riveted Steel
Length	61'6"
Beam	13'2"
Payload	60 Tons
Draft	4'5.5"
Weighed	Killaloe 1928
Engine	Bolinder E Type 15Hp
	Ford 5000 Diesel 1991
Home Base	Robertstown

Shruleen
Heritage Boat 53M

There were two 53M's and distinguishing their sometimes merged histories has been a real puzzle for years. To really confuse things neither boat had the traditional M Boat hull i.e. round bow and stern. From the records that are available, and information forthcoming from former crew, we can now separate with a fair degree of accuracy the two boats.

"The Shruleen" was the first 53M which was an odd build and a smaller boat than the standard Grand Canal Company boat. It was built in Portadown 1893 and was measured and weighed in 1894 in Killaloe. Length 60ft, Width 12ft 9ins, empty her stem was 6ft 5ins and her stern was 6ft 8ins. It was given the number 36 and operated for the Grand Canal Company (GCC). This was in a time prior to engines and the boat was towed by horses on the Canal and by steamers on the rivers. The introduction of the Bolinder

engine in 1911 signalled the demise of the GCC horse boats, which were retired over time. In 1928 a bronze stern gear was fitted for a Bolinder engine and the barge was to be transferred to the maintenance department. However for some reason this didn't happen and she was numbered 53M and put into the cargo fleet. It had a horse boat shape and was reportedly a fast boat. Its odd size was a draw back as she couldn't take a standard 50 ton load, and this resulted in her been exchanged for 98B in 1955.

According to Gerard Darcy in *Portrait of the Grand Canal* she was transferred to the maintenance department in 1955 and re numbered 93E. She went working on the Barrow with Jim Bolger and John Whelan. In 1962 Jim Gill from Graiguenamanagh worked her. They used her while erecting fencing, bank repairs, cutting back bushes etc. Eventually in 1968 she was brought to St. James's Street harbour where she was acquired by Rexie Rowan from Athy who changed her number back to 53M. On the way back down the canal in Inchicore she hit a submerged car which goes to show that the canal was considered a dumping ground in those days. Over the following years Rexie covered the hold and made some improvements and even brought her to the Shannon.

In 2004 Charlie and Bernie Mackey purchased her from Rexie who had retired and did not want to see her wasting away and was happy to know that she would continue to be based in Athy. In autumn

Shruleen, 53M, at St. James's St. Harbour

Courtesy — Shorthall Collection

2004 she was brought under her own power from Athy to Belmont and was left there for the winter. In spring 2005 it was moved to Shannon Harbour and into the dry dock where the hull was power washed and she was surveyed. She needed a fair amount of work and as Shannon Harbour dry dock was busy it was brought to Tullamore where a dry dock was available.

At Tullamore—2005

Over the winter of 2005 - 2006 re-plating work was done on the hull. Next step is a new superstructure.

Beside the Lady Annette (used as landing stage) in New Ross

Crew included—
Tom Connolly, Matt Smullen, Bonny McGrath both were supposed to have worked on her at one time. At another time Waxer Dunne was in charge with Jack "Porter" Farrell as engine man Paddy McNamee from Killina was deckman and Jim Press was greaser. In July 1942 Joe Connolly Shannon Harbour went to work on 53M to take up "Yank" Dunne's place. At that time Patsy Gordon from Harold's Cross was in charge with young Mick Lawlor.

Tom Lawlor took over as skipper in 1954 with John Conroy as his engineman.

Technical Details	
Reg. No.	53M
Built By	Portadown
Year	1893
Construction	Riveted Steel
Length	60'
Beam	12' 9"
Payload	46 Tons
Draft	4'
Weighed	Killaloe 1894 & 1913
Engine	Horse drawn up to 1928
	Bolinder 15hp
	BMC Sea Lord 6 Cyl Diesel
Steering	Tiller
Home Base	Athy

Courtesy — Shorthall Collection

Aiseiri
Heritage Boat 54M

54M was built in Dublin by Vickers (Ireland) Ltd in 1928. She operated on the Grand Canal carrying general cargo up to 1959 when the Grand Canal closed to commercial traffic. After the closure the boats were tied up in James's Street Harbour awaiting their eventual outcome. During this time the Maintenance Department had the pick of the fleet and some boats were transferred over to maintenance duties.

At that time Johnny Dunne and Paddy Doyle were both working aboard the engineering boat 91E which was originally

built in 1903 as Horse Boat 21, and became 1M with the installation of a Bolinder in 1912. The lads knew that the newer 54M had recently had her cabin refurbished and a new engine installed. This work was done shortly before the canal closure, so 91E was left in harbour and they took out 54M in its place.

According to Johnny they moved into the lap of luxury compared to what they had been used to. The pair used to stay on the boat during the week when they weren't near home. As an engineering boat 54M worked at cutting weeds during the summer, they moved lock gates, cleaning supplies, and occasionally used her as a mud boat when needed. In 1983 the Office of Public Works started to ferry the workers to site by van which put an end to the use of 54M for accommodation. New mud boats, which were shorter for turning and which were loaded and unloaded by digger, then came on line. This resulted in a number of older boats, including 54M, being retired from service and brought back to the harbour in Tullamore.

Post conversion on the Barrow

In 1995, 54M was selected as one of the barges to be leased out to a FAS community barge restoration project. 54M was rebuilt as a passenger carrying vessel and licenced to carry up to 50 passangers on the Grand Canal. The work was done by a group of FAS

A manpower manoeuvre brings 54M into the dry dock in Athy

his uncle Martin and Jim Nevin managed to go under Portumna Bridge, going down river with a load of porter, while the bridge was closed.

Dick's brother Todd Kearney also worked on 54M. In 1947 both Joe and Jack Daly from Banagher worked her after which Joe Connolly took over as skipper and Billy Colton was engineman, Joe Manning was deckman. When Billy left Joe Manning went as engineman and Pee Judge joined

workers in Athy between 1996 and 2000. After she was re-launched she was renamed "Aiseiri", the Irish word for "The Resurrection"

The barge was operated under the Athy Community Council who ran day and evening trips for a number of years after which she lay idle. Waterways Ireland have recently invested in the upgrade of 54M to a higher marine specification for use on the River Barrow, under the supervision of the Department of Marine.

Crew included—
It is alleged that Dick Kearney with

Aiseiri gets a preliminary clean-up. Notice the anti-vandal window covers. Unfortunately these could not prevent her later getting sunk twice by vandals opening the dock gate!

Waterways Ireland staff sealing the gate

as deckman. Around November of that year Pee Judge left, Joe Manning went back as deckman and Tom Connolly went as engineman.

Her last recorded crew were Tom Nolan (Master) Mick Nolan (Engineman) and Patrick Nolan (Deckman).

Heritage Boat 56M

When the commercial traffic closed on the canal in 1960, 56M was sold off by CIE at auction. Limerick Harbour Commissioners (LHC) were her next owners and used her for dredging work. We are lucky to have 56M with us today as when owned by LHC she was lost at sea, and remained so until the tides offered her up several years later. She broke free from her moorings in the waters around the Tarbert area during a strong storm and was swept out to sea. Over the next seven years the tides in the area swept her closer to shore until she eventually became salvageable in the late 1960's.

In the late 1960's Ronnie Gallagher was offered the barge for £100 but he had to salvage her himself. She was laden with sand and gravel and on low tides Ronnie and his son had to empty the hold until they were able to tow her with a small sailing boat back up the Shannon. Ronnie lived aboard her above Athlone at Shankeragh having fitted her with a timber superstructure. She passed through a number of hands over the next few years. Davy Dolan, son of the late Paddy Dolan, who lived aboard her on the quayside in Athlone, followed by Deckie Walshe, who is said to have paid £4,000 for her in 1978. After working on 56M with Deckie, Gerry Oakman of 29B was to become her next custodian, and in the early 1980's it was he who finished the steel superstructure with the characteristic stepped cabin-top and fitted her current engine. In 1982 Charlie Bishop a retired American naval officer who became enamoured with the Shannon became the proud owner of 56M. Charlie later met and got married to Janice Henry and they lived aboard until 1990.

They travelled to length and breadth of the Shannon, sometimes wintering in Athlone, sometimes in Shannon Harbour. They later sold 56M on to George and Eileen Leonard a retired couple. It was only advancing years that made George part with 56M in 1998. Eamonn Lindsay owned the barge for the next two years before Paul Egan and Mandy Henry (Janice's sister) the current owners bought her in April 2000. After buying her they immediately put it in for extensive rework in Shannon Harbour. The legacy of her time at sea became apparent

In Shannon Harbour with Charlie Bishop

In Portumna—2005

during her re-plating in 2001. The bow of the barge must have protruded out of the water more than the rest of the hull and with exposure to air, combined with the salt water, corroded the hull severely. Because of this her bow was re-sheeted in new steel for a length of 8ft topside and below the waterline. One curious detail was found when working on the bow. She was correctly numbered 56M on 3 of her panels but on the starboard bow the number 55M appeared, etched into the steel. It had been corrected to read 56M, but no doubt some worker must have been castigated for his error. 56M has been steered by the rudder off 4E for the last 30 years – it had been appropriated for use on 56M before 4E had been salvaged herself – thankfully Joe Treacy hasn't asked for it back!

Crew included—

The "Bishop" (Tom) Whelan was in charge of 56M around 1947-48 before he took out 66M. 56M was operated as a "Hack Boat"

when two brothers, Jack and Jim Bolff hired her out from the GCC for around two years that was circ 1949-50. Other people to work her were Chiny Thompson, Tom Bowers, Bert Conroy and Tom Connolly.

Technical Details	
Reg. No.	56M
Built By	Vickers (Ireland) Ltd
Year	1928
Construction	Riveted Steel
Length	61' 6"
Beam	13' 2"
Payload	62 Tons
Draft	4' 5.75"
Weighed	Killaloe 1928
Current Draft	3' 6"
Engine	Bolinder E Type 15Hp
	Ford Thames Trader 120Hp
Steering	Wheel with steering box of combine harvester & Tiller
Home Base	Hazelhatch

Maid of Allen
Heritage Boat 57M

57M was built for the Grand Canal Company in 1928 and was worked moving general cargo between Dublin, the Shannon and the Barrow for over 32 years. When the commercial traffic closed on the canal in 1960 she was sold off by CIE at auction. Drogheda Harbour Commissioners owned her for a number of years and then Drogheda Rowing Club and possibly an M. Rowan after that. Around 1973 Garda George Smith of Birr bought her.

At that time she was practically abandoned in Mornington with tide flowing in and out of holes in her hull. The Bolinder engine was still in her but they couldn't get it working. They filled the holes with concrete and

> *"They started from scratch, completely stripping her down to the hull and refitting her out as a houseboat"*

George had her towed by trawler to Dublin without incident. However they later ran into trouble going down the canal around Sallins and after a showdown with CIE,

57M in Waterford with working sailing ships   Courtesy — Shorthall Collection

they lifted her out of the Canal and brought her to Shannon Harbour by truck. She was put into dry dock where some basic repair work was carried out. George later sold to Greg Allen who owned pubs in Celbridge and Prosperous. It was Greg who named her the Maid of Allen. After converting her and replacing the engine he ran 57M as a trip boat on the canal around Robertstown and Sallins, before selling her on. She then moved into Dublin and operated as a trip boat on the Circular Line before been ordered to move outside the city limits by the Courts. 57M was moved to Clodalkin and was tied up around the 9th lock where she was vandalised and eventually set on fire. She was subsequently towed out to Hazlehatch and moored outside McEvoy's for a number of years before her current owners bought her. They started from scratch, completely stripping her down to the hull and refitting her out as a houseboat. She is currently moored in Sallins.

Courtesy — Shorthall Collection

Crew included—
While crews continuously swapped

between boats, we do know that in 1937 Paddy Connolly Shannon Harbour was greaser on 57M. Also there at that time were Willie and Harry Pender and Pat

Technical Details	
Reg. No.	57M
Built By	Vickers (Ireland) Ltd
Year	1928
Construction	Riveted Steel
Length	61' 6"
Beam	13' 2"
Payload	62 Tons
Max Draft	4' 5.75"
Weighed	Killaloe - 1928
Engine Original	Bolinder E Type 15Hp
Home Base	Sallins, Co Kildare

"Baker" Sheridan. Joe Connolly worked on 57M as deckhand when "Lady" Jack Dunican was Skipper, Willie "Sledger" Dunne was Engineman and John Donoghue, Greaser. In 1951 Tom Manning left 54M and joined 57M as engineman, with Mick Donnelon "in charge" (Skipper) at that time.

During conversion in Sallins

Heritage Boat 58M

Built in 1929 at Ringsend dockyard, Dublin, for the Grand Canal Company(GCC) and, like a lot of the McMillan boats, was used for the most part on the Barrow Navigation. She would have carried cargo from Dublin to Waterford with occasional ventures to the Shannon. As with all cargo boats she was calibrated for payload in Killaloe, on the 17th July 1929. This exercise involved the recording of boat draft at 2 ton intervals until she reached 4" 6". This information could be used to identify the payload carried by each barge at various locks and calculate tolls, etc.

After the closure of the Grand Canal in 1959, 58M was bought by Roadstone Ireland Ltd. who used her as a sand dredger on the Slaney for a number of years. She was eventually retired and abandoned in a sad state below Edermine Bridge in tidal waters on the river Slaney three miles below Enniscorthy town. Colm McGrath found 58M and later bought her, where she lay, from Roadstone in Enniscorthy where the Manager, Nicky Rackard, extracted the princely sum of £600. The boat was in a sad state being beached from the holes on both sides, which ran from bulkhead to bulkhead of the cargo hold. She had no

At New Ross with 35M

engine, the tiller handle was bent at right angles to the rudder but still had the steel hopper fitted in the cargo hold for carrying sand which was dredged from the river bed. Colm's first priority was to block the holes in the hull, straighten the tiller and fit a BMC 5.1 engine with a Borg Warner 2:1 Reduction gearbox.

On a Saturday morning in August 1978, 58M returned to life and set out at 6.00am from Enniscourthy reaching Wexford Bridge at 8.00am, around Hook Head at 16.00pm hours finally arriving at St. Mullins at 19.00pm. She then travelled on to Shannon

58M working on the Slaney

Courtesy — Shorthall Collection

Harbour and from there to Athlone. At Athlone the first priority was the removal of the sand hopper, bow cabin, engine room roof and 6" of deck on both sides of the hold. A new superstructure was installed and the conversion carried out then remains the same today. Colm lived on board 58M in Athlone from 1980 until 1987 and on board at Hazelhatch from 1987 until 1991. She is still in the McGrath Family who use 58M for family cruising on the Canal, the Shannon and were back down the Barrow in 2005.

Crew included—
As a young 16 year old deckhand Denis Rowan received the sum of 2 shillings and

six pence to bring 58M from Ringsend to James's St. harbour. Piery Bolger, Graiguenamagh, started work on 58M as a Greaser with his father in 1942 and with the exception of three weeks when he worked on 70M he spent all his 18 years on the canal on 58M until she was retired in 1960. Billy and Christy Bolger also worked on her. When Piery was the skipper he was known for always being in a hurry. He was continually last to leave but first to get there. Skipper Tom McGrath from Allenwood and his two sons Larry the driver/engineman and Paddy the deckhand were the last recorded crew members employed by CIE in January 1961.

Coming up from Graignamana

Countess Corinne
Heritage Boat 59M

*I*n May 1960, 59M left James's St. Harbour for the last time with a cargo of Guinness for the depot in Athy. She was sold off by CIE in the 1960's but wasn't converted until sometime in the 1970's. Her owners included D. O'Leary, Mr. Wilson, Dr. O'Callaghan and Dr. Oliver Connolly. She still had the original Bolinder Engine in 1993 when her current owner Phelim Nevin bought her. The original conversion was made of timber and felt and was in a pretty bad state so she was stripped right back to the hull and had a

Courtesy — Shorthall Collection

complete re-modeling with a steel super-structure and internal re-fit. This work took five years to complete. The Bolinder was replaced with a modern 120 horse power engine although it retained the original Bollinder cast iron prop. Work complete, Phelim set up home aboard 59M and even convinced Maria to join him as his wife. He

lived aboard her for about five years.

"Despite being the Captain's guest and gaining access to the bridge, Corinne calmly told the crew that it was not as good as Phelim's barge"

59M also proudly bears the name "Countess Corinne" after a little girl, Corinne Igoe, R.I.P., that Phelim had the privilege to know. Corinne fought a brave battle with Leukaemia, and had been given just a month to live. One of Corinne's last wishes was to travel on a "big ship". While 59M was not a big ship and still in the early stages of restoration, she was mobilized and set sail with almost fifty people aboard, including the Igoe family and friends. To this day, it is still one of the most enjoyable and memorable days on the barge. Two weeks later Corinne's wish to travel on a big ship came true, thanks to the "Make A Wish Foundation". Despite being the Captain's guest and gaining access to the bridge, Corinne calmly told the crew that it was not as good as Phelim's barge. Hence the barge now proudly bears the name "Countess Corinne".

59M is more than just a barge to Phelim, its part of his life that took blood, sweat and

59M at St. James's Street

New Ross did a spell with Chiny around the mid 40's. Joe Connolly, Mick "Yank" Dunne with Paddy "Waxer" and Paddy Brien did a term in her also in the 1940's. Jack Moore and Sean Donoghue were in her in 1948, Sean left and Willie Pender came in his place as Skipper. Willy was in her until 1951-52 when he got sick and went home for a while. Around 1953 Pat and Tommy Donoghue were on her as was Jack Gaffney for a while. They left and the Conroy's Mick and Todd (Bert) went to her in 1954.

tears to get her to her present condition. As far as it is possible to befriend a piece of steel, 59M is as an old friend who has repaid his efforts a hundred times over. Phelim's advice to anyone bitten by the barge bug, persevere, because it is only by persever-ance that you achieve and in achieving you will reap untold rewards.

Crew Included—
Her first skipper was Ned Pender. Tom Connolly, Shannon Harbour, who was a greaser on board during the 1936 greaser's strike Jim "Chiny" Thompson, Johnny Press, Paddy Adley and Amby Dwyer were in her together for a while. Chiny stayed the longest while the rest changed back and forth to other boats. Johnny Codd from

Technical Details	
Reg. No.	59M
Built By	Vickers (Ireland) Ltd
Year	1929
Construction	Riveted Steel
Length	61' 9"
Beam	13' 2"
Payload	60 Tons
Draft	4' 5.75"
Weighed	Killaloe 1929
Engines	Bolinder E Type 15Hp
	Ford D Series120hp
	6 Cylinder Diesel

During her second conversion

The last crew was John Coyne Skipper, Peter "Gurkyman" Anderson engineman and Sean Anderson was deckhand.

Clondra—2005

Eureka
Heritage Boat 60M

60M operated as a cargo boat on the Grand Canal from its launch in 1929 until the end of commercial traffic in 1959. She carried a range of cargos a lot of which were seasonal, such as grain, sugar beet, turf, and of course Guinness all year round.

In 1953 she was left in for a refit of new engine bed, a job that was not unusual on the M boats but could take some time depending on backlog in the workshops at any given time. It was not unknown for a boat to be out of operation for 2 to 3 years awaiting completion of works.

60M was sold off by CIE in the early sixties and ended up on the River Barrow at New Ross where she was used in the construction of the new bridge. She was later sunk and abandoned under the road bridge in New Ross. In 1973 Artie and Oonagh Corbett applied to and got permission from New Ross Harbour commissioners to raise 60M.

At this stage it was completely submerged and covered in silt and mud, even at low tide. Over the next few months Artie persevered in the recovery operation and even learned to dive. In 1974 60M was lifted from the bottom and moved to the side of the river. Unfortunately she slipped back into deep water so a second salvage operation was put into place after a few months when tides and weather were more favourable. The second recovery was more successful, with the 60M being successfully delivered across the river to the protection of shallow waters. Between 1975 and 1977 the Corbett's worked on restoring her, putting in an engine and converting the cargo hold into a living area.

In 1979 they brought 60M up the Barrow intent on getting to the river Shannon. Things on the Barrow navigation weren't all that great at this time and it took them a full year to complete the journey. Extensive weeds had clogged up the canals making passage by motor difficult. Some days they only managed to travel as little as a mile with Artie spending more time in the water than out. Another delay was waiting two months for a lock gate to be replaced before they could pass through. On the main line of the canal, the biggest delays were caused by plastic bags and shopping trolleys. In the mid to late 80's the original wheel house was demolished when coming down the river Shannon from Carrick on a flood. A new permanent

Courtesy — Shorthall Collection

Technical Details

Reg. No.	60M
Built By	Vickers (Ireland) Ltd
Year	1929
Construction	Riveted Steel
Length	61' 9"
Beam	13' 2"
Payload	62 Tons
Max Draft	4' 6"
Weighed	Killaloe - 1929
Engine	Bolinder E Type 15Hp
Home Base	Ferryhaven, Portumna

wheelhouse was built which gives 60M "Eureka" a very distinguishing profile but due to air draft restricts her movements to the Shannon.

Artie and Oonagh enjoyed a nomadic lifestyle on 60M for a number of years in their retirement. In the early nineties 60M got a more permanent berth when a group of boaters developed Ferryhaven at Portumna Bridge. However Ferryhaven is just a winter base, as Artie and Oonagh spent a lot of time in Dromineer and Athlone where they are both very active in sailing.

Crew Included—
Scotsman Connolly was her first Skipper. In the early 40's her crew was Martin and Paddy Connolly, Jim Flynn and Paddy McCormack. Tragically Paddy fell in to the canal one night between Daingean and Ballycommon and was drowned. Paddy Sullivan, Tom Nolan, Hairy Loonan and Paddy Sullivan were in her in the late 40's and tied up in 1948. Jim Maloney originally from Kildare but married in Banagher worked on 60M as did six of his sons at different times. They were Tom, Matt, Larry, Abie, Andy and Martin. Martin was known as "Tim" and also known as Sonny.

From 1948 to 1953 Matt Maloney, Andy Maloney and Jim Cox were her crew. She was tied up for about two years and when she came back after that her crew were Boney McGrath with his brother-in-law Jimmy Roche and Matt Duggan. About two years after Tony Dunne, Larry "Sleepy" Brien took her out. Tom Connolly of Shannon Harbour, Jimmy Nolan and "Capetown" Maher from Rathangan spent a while after that. Tom left to 56M. The last crew were Andy Maloney skipper, Tick Donelan engineman and Abie Maloney was deckhand.

An Murrough
Heritage Boat 61M

*I*t is believed that 61M was designed slightly different from the standard 'M' barge as an experiment. The GCC in an effort to boost freight profits decided to attempt to carry an extra layer of firkins of Guinness in the hold. Her freeboard is approximately 9" higher than the standard M Boat. Obviously the experiment was not successful, as they did not continue with the alteration to the boats that followed her.

CIE officially closed down for commercial trading in December 1959. However, they had to complete the building of storage sheds in Limerick for holding Guinness so fourteen boats were returned to service in January 1960. These boats worked until July 1960 when the canal was finally closed to commercial traffic. She was also used to recover equipment from the disused company depots along the Shannon and Grand Canal. For that six months she was crewed by three brothers Tom, Mick and Paddy Nolan (Rathangan).

Mr. McMullen and Jonathan P. T. Brooks bought the 61M from C.I.E in late 1960. Sometime between then and 1963 she was bought by Myles Digby, who had a plan to convert a number of barges into hire boats. These were to be self-contained barges suitable for anglers on a fishing holiday. However, this idea never materialised and she sank in Shannon Harbour. She was then sold to Jim Foley for £12–6s–0d. Jim Foley raised her and converted her using packing cases from the Ford Car plant in Cork. He used these along the bulkheads and deckheads, some of which are still there. Some of the deckheads and a skylight in the saloon were taken from the "Wayfarer". 61M, now converted, was towed down to Killaloe by the "Lady Beverley" to a berth outside the Lakeside Hotel where she remained as a home to the Foley family and their pet fox for seven years. Mike Roberts from Clondra bought her in 1970 for £2,000. He fitted a new engine and a wheelhouse and placed 2000 concrete bricks in to her, for ballast, that were later removed and replaced with mild steel railway lines. In 1981 an Aer Lingus pilot, Dermot Mowatt, bought her. He fitted her current engine and modern gearbox. He sold her to P.J. Norris on the 26th of February 1990. In 1992 Adair and John Leech her current owners bought 61M and named her after an ungainly fly, a Murrough. In the past 14 years An Murrough has navigated all

61M on the Nore

of the Shannon, the Erne, Grand Canal and the Three Sisters (the Barrow, the Nore and the Suir).

Crew included—

61M started trading May 1930 with Peter Duggan as her skipper. "Red" Ned Boland and Johnny Doyle of Allenwood was her Skipper for a number of years up to the mid 1940's. "Butcher" Cross and Eamon Pender worked with him. When Johnny left, Eamon became skipper. Butcher swapped with Jack Gaffney who took over as engineman. Jack left after some time and Willy Pender took his place. Matt Duggan worked with them as well. Paddy "Waxer" Dunne crewed from 1952 to 1954. His skipper was Red Mick O'Donoghue. Simon Mc Donald worked on her for just under a year. Bobsie Mann crewed and eventually became the skipper.

Jim Gill crewed in the 1950's with Eamon his brother Willie Pender. Larry Daly had also crewed her.

She was left in for repair in the early fifties, and on her return to service Jim Dunne and Pat Doyle took her out for a few months however the engine gave difficulties. Following further repairs, Eamon Pender went back to her as skipper from 1954 until December 1959. Jimmy Roche and Seamus Balph, both from Alenwood, also worked on her around this time .

Willie Flynn was a Deck Hand in 1957, he later became a Canal Maintenance Officer after 1960.

Technical Details	
Reg. No.	61M
Built By	Ringsend Dockyard Company
Year	1929
Construction	Riveted Steel
Length	61' 9"
Beam	13' 2"
Payload	60 Tons
Draft	4' 5.75"
Weighed	Killaloe 1929
Engines	Bolinder E Type 15Hp
	Perkins 6354

Heritage Boat 62M

62M was built for the Grand Canal Company and went straight away as a workboat on the Canal, Barrow and river Shannon carrying general cargos. In 1951 her crew were three brothers Willy Dunn with his brothers John "Seanie" and Paddy known as the "Waxer". On November 29th the Dunn's left Limerick with a load of cement partly in the hold and partly as deck cargo. 62M with 39M behind them were being towed up the tailrace by the St Patrick when 62M got caught in a cross flow and capsized. 62M sank almost straight away, luckily the crew all escaped and were picked up immediately by 39M. The crew on 39M that time was John Dunne, Joe Cox and Con Lenihan. 62M was left underwater in the tailrace for two and a half years while the ESB and CIE decided between them who were to remove it. In June 1953 CIE wrote to the ESB an extract from that later is quote: "owing to diminishing Canal traffic and this board's policy in relation thereto, the barge in question is no longer required and need not be replaced. The cost of raising it, estimated at £1,000, would represent a complete loss to us, in the circumstances I am to enquire if the board would agree to leave this barge where it is". The ESB response was that they wanted it removed as it was an obstruction in the channel. In the end CIE gave the boat over to the ESB for their own salvage.

In June 1954, ESB successfully lifted 62M by winching her up between two of its own Dumb Barges (ESB No1 & ESB No2). John Dunn was sent down by CIE and when the boat was lifted he was allowed to go into the cabin and retrieve his purse which still contained £90 lost. The full story of lifting 62M was told in an ESB magazine and re printed in the IWAI book published in 1996 to commemorate the 25th Shannon Harbour Canal Boat Rally.

Courtesy — Shorthall Collection

After being lifted it was towed to Killaloe and dry docked at the Pier Head, the Bolinder engine was overhauled and the barge put back into service as a work boat attached to Civil Works Maintenance Section of the ESB at Ardnacrusha. In the 1980's it had a steel cabin fitted at the tiller area to act as a windbreak and also house the control panel of the engine. The boat has had some repairs to the steel plating over the years and has just undergone some work with a safety handrail around the tiller area and a toilet has also been installed in the forward section of the hold area.

62M being raised in 1986

and Tom Maloney from Banagher also worked on her. In November 1951 her crew were three brothers Willy Dunn with his brothers John "Seanie" and Paddy known as the "Waxer".

ESB crew—
The following is a list of some of the people that have worked on 62M since 1954. Sonny McEvoy with Michael Hogan and Paddy Healy, Mickey Connelly with John McEvoy and Pat Nash. Mossy Riordan, Mickey Fitzpatrick, Ned Columby, Paddy Flynn and Ritchie Hackett.

ESB has used the barge on various projects as a work boat, carrying materials up and down the Headrace at Ardnacrusha on grouting operations, drilling operations and concrete plating maintenance. It would also have been used for work in the Portumna and Athlone areas.

62M was actually sunk and salvaged for a second time in the Tailrace, just downstream of the Navigation Locks at Ardnacrusha, in July 1986. 63M along with Ken Simmons was involved in that salvage operation.

Technical Details	
Reg. No.	62M
Built By	Vickers (Ireland) Ltd
Year	1929
Construction	Riveted Steel
Length	61' 9"
Beam	13' 2"
Payload	60 Tons
Max Draft	4' 5.5"
Weighed	Killaloe - 1929
Engines	Bolinder E Type 15Hp taken out of 27M
	Lister Marine Diesel Type 44.25hp 1975
	Vetus Marine Diesel 65hp 2006
Home Base	Killaloe

Many thanks to Senan McEvoy for his help in putting this together.

Crew included—
Her first skipper was Peter Duggan. Crews on canal boats constantly changed so its very hard to keep track of who exactly worked on each boat but from the memory of the men that worked them we know that Joe Connolly from Shannon Harbour worked on her at one time. Paddy "Bogyman" Kelly with his two sons Paddy "Paugeen" Kelly and Johnny were a crew on her another time. Tom Connolly from Graignamanagh, Larry Daly from Shannon Harbour

62M—May 2006

Heritage Boat 63M

She was built for the Grand Canal Company and operated as a trading boat on the Canal, Shannon and the Barrow until the CIE closed up operations in 1959.

In the winter of 1947, 63M rolled over and sank across the buttresses of Mathew Bridge in Limerick. Tom Maloney and Sam Cox were crewing her at the time. They had left the lock at the Canal Depot and were heading for Dublin back up the Abbey River with a load of empties. At Athlunkard Bridge (O'Dwyer's Bridge) the engine stalled. Furious attempts were made to re-start the engine as the boat was carried back down the Abbey River with the flow. Eventually she got stuck across the buttress of Mathew Bridge. The crew were immediately rescued from the boat by ropes down from the bridge, while the boat eventually lost its battle with the current, turned over and sank. She was left there for the winter and was raised by the Canal Company the following summer.

"The crew were immediately rescued from the boat by ropes down from the bridge, while the boat eventually lost its battle with the current, turned over and sank"

Like a lot of the boats she was sold off at auction by CIE in 1960. We don't know who bought her but she was later owned by Galway scrap dealer Christy Dooley. The story goes that she was used to bring a Caterpillar earth mover to the Aran Islands for a contractor in the early 1970's. Ken Simmons purchased her in 1976 and brought her from Galway to Killaloe by truck. Ken installed a hydraulic crane on the bow and accommodation over half of the cargo hold. Part of the fit out included a bath which was top shelf for the day. He then used her for years doing dredging work around the Shannon

63M at Shannon Harbour—May 2006

and was even involved in the recovery of 62M when she sank in 1986. In 1990 Ken sold her on to Derg Line cruisers in Killaloe where she was used in the building of jetties. Derg Line leased her to Liam O'Flynn for a while after which she was laid up in the mid 90's and spent a couple of years on the bank awaiting repairs when Liam purchased her. 63M is still in continuous use doing maintenance work which makes her one of the last canal work boats.

Courtesy — Shorthall Collection

Technical Details

Reg. No.	63M
Built By	Vickers (Ireland) Ltd
Year	1930
Construction	Riveted Steel
Length	61' 6"
Beam	13' 2"
Payload	62 Tons
Max Draft	4' 6"
Weighed	Killaloe - 1930
Engine Original	Bolinder E Type 15Hp
Home Base	Lough Derg

Courtesy — Shorthall Collection

Crew included—
Christy "Nigger" Cross was Skipper on her at one stage with Jack "Flinter" Bagnell as deckman and. "Banagher" Jack was engineman. Joe Connolly from Shannon Harbour was engineman on her for a short while also. In 1947 Tom Maloney and Sam Cox

The Bishop Whelan
Heritage Boat 66M

On September 29th 1965 Padraic O' Brolchain found himself to be the proud owner of 66M when he bought her at auction. He was furnished with a lock pass for the 32 locks to Carlow and an instruction that the barge had to be got out of the harbour within a week. The Bolinder engine was in situ less most of the important bits that made it work. Within the week they had got together a team armed with a lock key, tow ropes, a 3hp

Courtesy — Shorthall Collection

Crossing the Suir at Waterford with 31M

outboard, and various slashers, saws, grabs etc. Their first day's trip got them from the James's St. to under the Naas road bridge at the 3rd lock. The outboard, clamped to the tiller was a success and with manual effort on ropes they got her the next day to the Guinness filter beds where by arrangement they wintered. The following spring they mounted a tractor engine on the roof

of the engine compartment and with a belt drive to the Bolinder flywheel they headed off to Carlow. They moved her at week-ends only so it took all summer to get there. She sank a few times along the way and with weeds on the canal they often got only two or three miles in a day. When they got to Carlow they lifted 66M on to the bank to patch the hull which had over 30 visible holes. The Bolinder was removed and replaced with a tractor engine. A steel superstructure erected which was a novelty in those days as most people were using timber and felt.

Finally in 1973, 66M was ready, although not fully converted it was habitable and she was moved to the 17th lock. In 1976 she was taken on the Shannon for the first time, freshly painted with no number or name. On the return trip to Dublin, several lock keepers enquired as to her number and when 66M was called out their response was always "Ah J----s the Bishop Whelan" (the last skipper associated with 66M) Hence she was christened .

The "Bishop Whelan" has traveled extensively attending many rallies over the years. She is now owned by Padraic's brother Aongus and underwent a major refit plus the addition of a wheel-house in 2003. During this refit the familiar steel shutters over the windows were removed.

Crew Included—
1936- Her first Skipper was Dan Logan.
1939 - Ned Kelly was Skipper, Sean Tierney Deckman, Tom Coyne engine-

Courtesy — Shorthall Collection

man and "Swither" Sullivan (Dublin) was greaser. 1940's - Jack Connolly, Johnny Press (Percival) and Tom Bower. 1947 - 59 Tom "Bishop" Whelan was Skipper. His sons John, Pat and Tom all came to came to work with him at some time. Pat Whelan and Oliver McDonald were crewing to 1959. 66M was one of the fourteen boats put back on the Canal for six months in 1960. At that time its crew were Addy Danger (Aungier) and John Joe Mc Dermott.

66m with new wheelhouse

Seano
Heritage Boat 67M

67M had a working life of 24 years before she was sold off at auction by CIE when the canal trade ceased in 1960. Like all M boats she would have carried general cargo to all parts of the inland navigation. Sometime after she was sold off her Bolinder engine was removed and replaced with a petrol engine. She did however maintain her original working layout and could be seen tied up disused in Hazelhatch for at least fifteen years. Gay Boylan who owned her at that time sold her in 1997 to Charlie Dunn who set about a total refit and conversion of the hold area. Charlie installed an 80hp Ford diesel engine and renamed her "The Hazel". In 2001 Jimmy and Margaret Sexton purchased her. Jimmy an ex Irish Navy shipwright set about a total refit of the barge. The interior stripped and replaced, completely rewired, installed a reconditioned 120 six cylinder engine, replaced the port holes along the side with bigger windows, put on a new coach roof and built a wheelhouse.

At Shannon Harbour—2000

The renovation is almost complete and next year when its painted he intends to re-name her "Seano" in memory of his father.

Crew included—
Jim Moore was her first Skipper. Jim Gill worked on 67M in 1946, at that time his father Paddy was in charge with his brother Tom and Kit Connolly. Tom Connolly, Paddy Coyne, Tommy Coyne, John Coyne, Tony Murphy, Dinny Roe, Ned Neill, Jack and Jimmy Nolan and Joe Connolly all worked on her at other times.

Courtesy — Shorthall Collection

Technical Details	
Reg. No.	67M
Built By	Vickers (Ireland) Ltd
Year	1936
Construction	Riveted Steel
Length	61' 6"
Beam	13' 1.5"
Payload	60 Tons
Draft	4' 5.5"
Weighed	Killaloe 1936
Engine	Bolinder E Type 15Hp
	Petrol Engine
	80Hp Ford Diesel
	120Hp 6 Cylinder Diesel
Home Base	Hazelhatch

37M on the Grand Canal in Dublin

The Lora Marie
Heritage Boat 68M

Courtesy — Shorthall Collection

*W*hen the canal finally closed in 1960, 68M wasn't sold off but was kept by CIE for maintenance purposes. She was used as a Mud Boat (also known as clay or gravel boat) from the mid to late 1960's to 1980. Technically when she worked as a maintenance boat on the canal she should have been re-numbered to an "E" (Engineering) boat, but the re-numbering didn't continue after the commercial activity had ceased on the canals. In 1980 prior to her being laid up her cabin was stripped out in Athy dry dock as she was destined for a fit out like 51M, the carpenters boat. For some reason CIE changed their minds and that never happened. Her Bolinder was removed and sold, it ended up in England, while the hull was left to rust away with a number of other disused barges partially submerged in the Grand Canal at Ballycommon. A year or so later because of vandalism these boats were moved to Tullamore Harbour for safe keeping were 68M sank and remained under water until August 1993.

In 1991 when the first Waterways series, 45M, was being made, the inside of the hull of 68M was filmed underwater in Tullamore Harbour and was shown in the series.

In 1993 68M was raised by its new owner Dick Kearney. Dick with the help of his sons Declan and Paul then towed her to Lowtown where it remained tied to the canal bank under the watchful eye of Paddy "Waxer" Dunne until she was purchased by Gerry Burke in August 1995. As there was no engine fitted she was sailed down the Canal and Shannon with two outboard engines mounted on to a bracket on the tiller. With no dry dock facilities on Lough Derg, she was pulled ashore with tractors in December of 1995. In March 1996 she was sandblasted and painted and over the following months the bilges were re-plated on both sides. She was re launched (rolled back into the water) on June 9th, and the current engine was fitted the following week. She was used extensively in 1996 attending the 25th Shannon Harbour Canal Boat Rally and the Lough Derg Rally. While the living conditions were basic, with the crew sleeping on boards in the cargo hold under a leaky canvas cover, everybody had lots of fun. The following years saw the superstructure added, with twenty tonne of loose stone added as ballast. Work stopped each the summer while the crew enjoyed themselves. The winter (97/98) saw the addition of the wheelhouse and cabins started to appear down below. Voyages for 1998 included trips to Belturbet and back as well as attending the Shannon Harbour & Derg Rallies. The following winter 98/99 saw the completion of the interior fitting out.

Over the past few years 68M has been to

Dublin twice, the first time was to attend the World Canal Conference and the official launch of the Heritage Boat Association (HBA). To mention a few other destinations, it's been to Limerick a number of times, as well as the Erne, Belleek, Boyle and Lough Allen and in 2005 we went down the Barrow to New Ross, the Suir to Waterford & Carrick on Suir, Inistiogue on the Nore and did some estuary cruising.

M Boats are often incorrectly referred to as Guinness boats, but having a liking for the stuff myself the interior is full of Guinness memorabilia. A keg of draught is kept aboard a few times a year and if that wasn't enough a few years ago we painted her Black and Cream.

Crew included—
"Old Gent" McDermott (Daingean) was her first Skipper, Dick Kearney was a greaser in 1939, at that time the crew were Paddy Connolly (Killina), Tom Hilbert (Ballyteague) and Gannon Melia (Ticknevin). Amby Dwyer (Newcastle), Tom Doonican (Pollagh) and Banagher Tom (Tom Carroll), Banagher Jack (Tom's brother), Jack Kearney (Dicks brother), "Baker" Sheridan (Littletown) was Skipper in the early 40's after that Gannon Melia was skipper from circ 1943-44 to 1946-47. Paddy Kearney (Dicks brother) and Bill Cox worked on her circ 1947. Anthony Donohue (Allenwood/Killaloe) was skipper when Tom Nolan took over from him around 1948. At that time Peter Brien was engine man and Tom's brother Paddy was deck hand. Tom stayed in charge of her until circa 1953, when Tom left his brother Paddy took over as skipper and his other brother Jack joined as deckhand.

Peadar Boland (Robertstown) worked on her for a short while in the early fifties. Peter Brien left in late 1954 and Tommy Anderson (Allenwood/Carlow) replaced him as engine man. Paddy Nolan was skipper for about eighteen months and was

replaced by "Gurkyman" (Peter) Anderson (Tommy's brother). Around 1955 Paddy Doherty (Graiguenamagh) and his two sons John & Paddy took out 68M and worked her until she was laid up with all the other CIE boats when c anal operations were halted at Christmas 1959. In January 1960, 68M was brought back into service for six months to help in the decommissioning of the canal system and to continue drawing Guinness to Limerick. 'Waxer' (Paddy) Dunne was skipper, Tom Connolly was engine man and Tom "Mocus" Farrell (Ballyteague) was deck hand.

As a Maintenance Boat—
Willy Anger, Tommy "Skranny" Kelly (Rathdangan) and Kit Moran (Robertstown) were her crew from 1968 -72. Willy left in 1972 and Mick Donaher (Umeras Bridge) replaced him, that crew stayed in place until 1980.

Technical Details	
Reg. No.	68M
Built By	Vickers (Ireland) Ltd
Year	1936
Construction	Riveted Steel
Length	61' 6"
Beam	13' 1.5"
Payload	60 Tons
Draft Loaded	4' 5 1/2"
Draft Empty	1' 6"
Weighed	Killaloe 1936
Current Draft	3' 3" Ballasted
Engine	Bolinder E Type 15Hp 120hp Perkins S6M
Home Base	Lough Derg

68M on the Suir—2005

The Mason's Boat
Heritage Boat 69M

69M was one of eight new canal boats built by Vickers (Ireland) Ltd. for the Grand Canal Company in 1936. She sailed throughout the navigation carrying general cargo including Guinness for the next 20 years and was one of the boats kept in service after the closure of the canals to commercial traffic in 1959. She was subsequently transferred to the Maintaince Dept. where she was used as a

deckman in the early 1940's when Paddy "Bustin" Carroll was skipper and Jack Finnegan was the engineman. Joe acted as skipper in 1942 while his brother Paddy was out sick. The crew then was Micky Connolly (Graig) as engineman, Jim Nevin was deckhand and Seanie Madden was greaser and for a while Paddy "Brownie" Dolan from Banagher was second greaser. When Paddy came back Joe went back to deck man and Jim Nevin left the crew.

Joe told a story in "Through the Locks" that they were loading for Waterford one day and "Bustin" wouldn't give in and admit that he didn't know the way to Waterford so he just left the job and Pat Cahill went in charge. When they got back from Waterford "Bustin" came back. Tom Connolly, Peter Coyne, Micky Connolly, John McGrath, Christy Fitzpatrick and Waxer Dunne all worked on 69M at one time.

Courtesy — Shorthall Collection

clay boat for canal and bank repairs until 1990, when the new smaller clay boats came on stream, after which she gracefully retired from service to Tullamore Harbour where she currently lies sunk to the deck level. 68M remains in original serviceable condition and remains part of the Waterways Ireland fleet.

Crew included—
Joe Connolly, Shannon Harbour, was a temporary

Sunk at Tullamore Harbour

James's Street Harbour—57M, 72M & 76M

Lady Avalon
Heritage Boat 70M

*A*fter a good working life of 24 years, 70M wasn't sold off at the first auction of boats in 1960 but was used as a maintenance boat on the Canal. Then in September 29th 1965, CIE had a sale of Canal Barges by Public Auction at St James's Street Harbour. The barges for sale that day were 31M, 44M, 66M, 67M, 70M, and 76M.

70M was bought at the auction by John Barker from Glenageary. She was later sold to Gerard Brady and Jeremiah Deasy. At one stage she was converted as a Bar/Restaurant. In November 1975 they sold her to Sheelagh Maunsell and her husband. In their ownership she was known as the "Lady Avalon". After that Bill Pigot bought her in 1983 and lived on her at Connaught Harbour in Portumna until some months before he died in 1992. By his will, Bill left 70M to his godchildren David Pigot Jnr. and

Andrea Martin. Andrea, not long afterwards bought out David and became the sole owner. And it was from Andrea that Geoff and Dick Lovegrove, her current owners bought her in 1994. She was still lying in Connaught Harbour in a pretty sorry state although she had been converted (and apparently won the prize for the best conversion at the first Shannon Rally in

> *"when settled weather was forecast in August, they brought her down by sea to Waterford Harbour and up the Barrow to New Ross"*

1971), she had fallen into disrepair and was in need of TLC. Undeterred, by this the two brothers eagerly set forth about doing her up. They installed a reconditioned diesel engine and a new gearbox. Her bilges were in a bad state so they replaced all of the bilge on the port side and most of the bilge on the starboard side. They fitted a new steering system and brought her up the canal to Ringsend where they spent the next four years giving her a complete refit.

Courtesy — Shorthall Collection

By the summer of 1998 she was ready for action, but there was a problem leaving Ringsend because the 9th Lock was thought to be unsafe and no traffic was allowed through. Frustrated at being stuck in Ringsend, when settled weather was forecast in August, they brought her down by sea to Waterford Harbour and up the Barrow to New Ross. Aongus O'Brolchain

"they explored the Nore and the Suir before returning via the Barrow to the Shannon where she is once again berthed at Portumna"

and Peter Gray came as crew for the journey which is another story in itself. They spent the following two years at St Mullins from where they explored the Nore and the Suir before returning via the Barrow to the Shannon where she is once again berthed at Portumna.

Crew Included—
The original crew were Willie Pender as Skipper (he became the lock keeper at

At Portumna

The following year Michael Lawlor, aged 18, joined the crew as Greaser. The rest of the crew were Pat Pender (Skipper), Andy Fawcett (engine man) and Andy Cross was Deckhand. In the early 1940s the Connolly family began to be involved as crew and in 1944 the crew were Jim "Devil" Connolly (Skipper), Jack "Porter" Farrell (Engineman), Chris "Kit" Connolly (Deckhand) and Thos. "Scudge" Tanner was the Greaser. During her working life, Billy Cotton, Dick Kearney, Jack Kearney, Paddy Kearney, Willy Buckley and Jim Gill all worked on 70M at different times. Her last crew before the canals were closed was Tom Connolly (Skipper), his brother John was Engineman and his brother-in-law Nessan Redmond was Deckman.

Ticknevin), Harry Pender as Engineman, Pat Sheridan was Deckhand and Jackie Herbert was the Greaser.

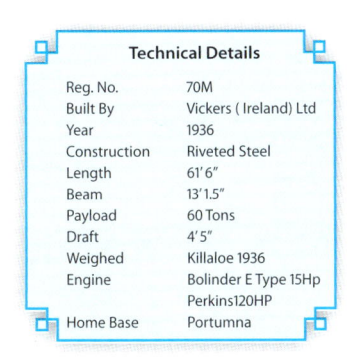

Technical Details	
Reg. No.	70M
Built By	Vickers (Ireland) Ltd
Year	1936
Construction	Riveted Steel
Length	61' 6"
Beam	13' 1.5"
Payload	60 Tons
Draft	4' 5"
Weighed	Killaloe 1936
Engine	Bolinder E Type 15Hp Perkins120HP
Home Base	Portumna

Heritage Boat 71M

Built by Vickers 71M was one of the last batch of M barges delivered to the Grand Canal Company in 1937. She, like the other M barges, carried general cargo throughout the navigation but had the had the distinction of taking the shortcut over Bestfield Weir on the Barrow when the river was in flood. Tom Connolly was the skipper accompanied by his brother John ("Squaw") and brother in law Dick "Nessan" Redmond. When the Canal was closed down 71M was sold at auction by CIE to Betty Williams in 1960 for £125. She was brought down the Barrow to Waterford with Hugh Malet ("Voyage in a Bowler Hat") amongst the crew. Hugh was travelling all the waterways of Ireland, researching for his book. The Williams'

lived on an island near Waterford and for many years 71M made the trip up to the Mill in Waterford on the rising tide and home again on the ebb, fetching seed and fertiliser and delivering grain after the harvest. She was sold on in 1966 to Waterford Harbour Commissioners who used her for work on the new bridge. She later sank and was abandoned on a sand bank in the estuary for sometime before been raised and moved to New Ross where she again ended up on a sand bank in the salt water.

Somehow she made her way to Athy, where she was holed and sank yet again. About Christmas 1971 she was acquired by Liam Covney who set about raising her with the help of Tom Carbery, George Spiers, Donal Murphy, Michael Rowan and the Athy Fire Brigade. Tom and Yvonne Stewart acquired her shortly afterwards and set about converting her to a house boat at the jetty just above Leeson Street Bridge in Dublin. The side decks were removed which gives her a distinctive look outside with a roomier feel inside. Tom used her extensively in the early seventies. After Tom's death she was sold to her current owners Brian and Sally Crawford in November 1986 who apart from removing

Courtesy — Shorthall Collection

some of the more obvious fire hazards (polystyrene ceiling tiles) - made few changes until 2002/3. By 2002 the ravages of her time on the sand banks in salt water were obvious so a major plating job was called for. After that was done she got a complete refit of the interior, including central heating.

Crew included—
Her first skipper was Billy Bulger and he spent a good few years on her. In the early 1940's Willy Dunne, Tosh Cross, Shonie Dunne, Paddy "Waxer" Dunne and at one stage Ned Dunne were on her. Willy, Shonie and "Waxer" stayed on her until they left to take out 62M.

In the late 40's Dick Kearney, Billy Colton and Paddy Kearney were on her. When they were told that they were to be tied up (no work for the boat), they all went their different ways. Dick left the canal altogether and never returned. After that Jack Kearney, Paddy Bagnall and John Coyne were on her. When they left her in, Tom Connolly was in charge of 37M. John "Squaw" Connolly

came back from England, Tom left 37M and the two of them with their brother in law Dick "Nessan" Redmond took out 71M. After that were Pat Doyle (Skipper), Mick Tierney (Engineman) and John Doyle (Deckhand). Pat and Mick took retirement, John moved to the 55M for the final year. Then Andy Maloney with his brother Abie Maloney and Tick Tom Donnellan took her out. Andy was in charge and held her for a while until near the end of 1959 he went back to 60M.

Other crew members that were supposed to have worked on her were Mick Conroy, Billy Clinton and Joe Connolly. Christy "Gent" McDermott was supposed to have been skipper on her for a while and Paddy McDermott was a greaser at one stage.

Technical Details	
Reg. No.	71M
Built By	Vickers (Ireland) Ltd
Year	1936
Construction	Riveted Steel
Length	61' 6"
Beam	13' 1.5"
Payload	61 Tons
Draft	4' 5.25"
Weighed	Killaloe 1936
Engine	Bolinder E Type 15Hp
	Ford Thornycroft 6.25lt
Gearbox	Borg Warner Hydraulic
	3-1 reduction gearbox
Propeller	30" x 18" 3 blades
Home Base	Lough Derg

Heritage Boat 72M

72M was one of eight new boats the Grand Canal Company commissioned from Vickers in 1936. After a productive working life on the canal it was sold off at auction by CIE after the canal closed down in 1959. Her work days weren't over though as she was later used as an Engineering boat. The company that bought her were Cementation & Site Investigation Work and they used 72M when putting down sidings and pilings as well as other projects that they did along the Shannon and the Canal. After that 72M lay derelict in Ringsend Basin for nine years before she was bought by her current owners Ronny and Mary Byrne in 1998. While its not of nautical interest, one piece of history

The Byrnes with the help of Richard and Mary Swayne spent the next six years working on her in Ringsend. They built and fitted out the superstructure and installed an engine. After that she made her first pow-

Courtesy — Shorthall Collection

ered journey in fifteen years on May Day 2004. In June of that year after the Dublin Rally 72M along with a fleet of other Canal Boats (Barges) that had been in Dublin for the rally made her way down the canal to Shannon Harbour. In 2005 while in Shannon Harbour a new prop shaft was fitted and her bilges were completely replated. While not fully finished she is now ready to start re-exploring places that she hasn't been to in 50 years.

is that U2 used 72M in their video "Gloria" (a single from their 1981 album October). The video was shot with the band performing on top of the barge in the middle of Ringsend Basin.

Crew Included—
Its first Skipper was Paddy Blight who as far as we can determine was on her for a good while. In the early 1940's the crew at one stage was Joe Connolly from

Shannon Harbour, engineman. In the mid 1940's "Banagher" Jack (Carroll) worked on her with Tom Nolan. 72M was the only other Canal boat on Lough Derg on Dec 1st 1946, the day that the 45M sank. She left Portumna that morning after early Mass before the storm got too bad. On her way down the lake they hugged the Galway and Clare shore and were tied up in Killaloe before the St. James and the 45M left Garrykennedy. While Tom Nolan went home for a few months Banagher Jack stayed on 72M until around 1948 when he went to 43M.

Johnny and Mick Donoghue and Anthony Kennedy were in 75M. Their engine bed was bad and the engine was jumping out of her on the upper lake (Lough Ree), so they went to 72M and stayed on her until 1951. Jimmy Fitzgerald of Graiguenamagh and "Lucky" Roche went to her after that. Jim spent about two years in her before going on to 46M. Willie Pender and Jim Lenihan were the last to work on her. Other men that were reported to have worked on 72M were Tom Bowers, Dick Kearney, Willy and Paddy Pender. At another time Jim Leeson was in charge and "Tinch" Sales as deckman. Gerry Kelly also worked on 72M as a deck man.

72M at Ringsend—2004

Technical Details	
Reg. No.	72M
Built By	Vickers (Ireland) Ltd
Year	1936
Construction	Riveted Steel
Length	61' 6"
Beam	13' 1.5"
Payload	60 Tons
Draft Loaded	4' 5"
Weighed	Kill aloe 1936
Engine	Bolinder E Type 15Hp
	130Hp Ford Diesel
Home Base	Shannon Harbour

72M, passing through Dolphins Barn, a working boat in the 1970's

The Millicent
Heritage Boat 73M

73M was built by in Dublin for the Grand Canal Company by Vickers in 1936. She worked on the Grand Canal, Shannon and Barrow carrying general cargo which included porter. It's the porter connection which leads to these boats being incorrectly referenced as Guinness Boats.

73M was sold at auction in Shannon Harbour in 1969 by CIE when they were disposing of some of the remaining fleet of canal boats. She was bought by Joe Giffen from Belfast for £60. She still had her Bolinder engine in and would have had been an empty hull as originally designed for cargo carrying with crew's quarters at the bow. Joe had great plans, but never got around to using her much or converting her for living on. John Weaving's barge, 'The Talisman' also known as, 'The Peter Farrell' had a pile driver fitted on one side of her, which he used for building harbours. When he used it his barge would lean over so he would regularly borrow 73M to tie to the opposite side to keep her steady.

Gerry Oakman came across her in 1974 lying in the old canal beside Carrick-on-Shannon. He found out who owned her, and thought about buying her for several months.

Meanwhile Noreen Griffen was looking for a barge and came asking Gerry who sent her to look at 73M. She couldn't get the money together but suggested Gerry should buy it anyway. Joe was looking for £750. Gerry

> *"He brought her up the Grand Canal to Dublin around 1976 and purchased a bar licence for her. He then took people on short trips along the canal in the Baggot Street and Mespil Road area"*

scraped up the £750 but then talked him down to £700. It cost the other £50 to get John Weaving to tow her to Athlone. Gerry fitted a modern diesel engine from a

Courtesy — Shorthall Collection

truck and anytime he got some money together, he would spend it on steel or timber for the conversion. He slowly welded on the current superstructure and fitted out the inside. He brought her up the Grand Canal to Dublin around 1976 and purchased a bar licence for her. He then took people on short trips along the canal in the Baggot Street and Mespil Road area. He had to give up this venture after a year as Dublin was just too

Courtesy — Shorthall Collection

He travelled all over the Shannon with 73M for holidays and often took in a rally or two along the way

dangerous to keep a boat so he took it back to the quay wall in Athlone.

Gerry lived on her there while he converted 56M and then 29B. He travelled all over the Shannon with 73M for holidays and often took in a rally or two along the way. In the late eighties he sold her to Ronnie Gallagher who eventually brought it to Hazlehatch. In the mid 1990's Ronny sold it to Paul McCormack who lived on it for a few years. The current owner has her since around 2000.

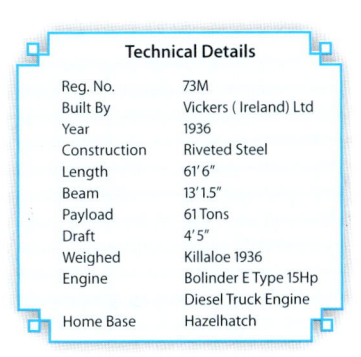

Technical Details

Reg. No.	73M
Built By	Vickers (Ireland) Ltd
Year	1936
Construction	Riveted Steel
Length	61' 6"
Beam	13' 1.5"
Payload	61 Tons
Draft	4' 5"
Weighed	Killaloe 1936
Engine	Bolinder E Type 15Hp Diesel Truck Engine
Home Base	Hazlehatch

Heritage Boat 74M

74M worked on the Canal, Shannon and the Barrow carrying general cargo until commercial traffic ceased in 1959. She was sold by C.I.E c1969 at the Shannon Harbour Auction and bought by New Ross Harbour Commissioners. After moving to New Ross, she was converted to a dredger with the cargo hold modified as a hopper and a hydraulic crane fitted on her bow. She

74M—2006

Prior to conversion—1997

worked for some time as a dredger in New Ross. Roadstone Ireland, Enniscorthy later bought 74M and used her to dredge sand on the Slaney. After that she was operated privately by one of the Roadstone men who used her for dredging work in Wexford town. Matt Driscoll bought her around 1996 and transported her by road on a low loader to Banagher. She was moved then to Shannon Harbour and dry docked for about a year. During that time her bilges were re-plated and the hopper was taken out of the hold. Gerry Oakman bought her from Matt and fitted a new engine. He owned her for a year or so and eventually sold it on to its current owners Cathy Dwane and Mark Becker.

Over the past three years 74M has been transformed as part of its conversion to a pleasure craft.

Crew included—
Dick Kearney, Paddy and Willy Pender, Jim Gill, Tom Connolly, Jim (Seamus) Farrell, Willy Roche's and "Waxer" (Paddy) Dunne all worked on 74M at one time. In early 1940 the crew included "Banagher" Tom (Carroll), Joe Connolly Shannon Harbour was also deckman later on that year for a short time when he replaced Larry Daly who was out with a busted finger. That time Christy "Gent" McDermott was in charge Tom (Joe's brother) was engineman and Paddy McDermott was greaser.

Technical Details	
Reg. No.	74M
Built By	Vickers (Ireland) Ltd
Year	1936
Construction	Riveted Steel
Length	61' 6"
Beam	13' 1.5"
Payload	61 Tons
Draft Loaded	4' 5"
Weighed	Killaloe 1936
Current Draft	3' 6"
Engine	Bolinder E Type 15Hp
	Perkins 6354
Home Base	Lough Derg

Heritage Boat 75M

75M was built in 1937 and has the distinction of being the last canal boat built by Vickers. Tom Doyle worked on her as a greaser in 1939 at that time Jack Byrne from Tullamore was in charge with Dick Pender as driver and Paddy O'Brien from Ballycommon as deckhand. Jock Byrne from Tullamore also

stations. For that last six months Jimmy Dean (Killaloe) was the Skipper, Anthony Kennedy (Allenwood/Ballina) was the Driver/Engineman.

She was purchased back in the 1960's from CIE by Mick Tully a farmer of Portrunny in Roscommon. Mick brought her to Lough Ree and used to start the Bolinder and take her for the odd trip around Lough Ree. Mick died in 2004 and his son now owns it. 75M is unique in that she is one of the two remaining unconverted boats still with Bolinder's in them, the other one being 45M.

75M—2006

Technical Details	
Reg. No.	75M
Built By	Vickers (Ireland) Ltd
Year	1937
Construction	Riveted Steel
Length	61'6"
Beam	13'1.5"
Payload	61 Tons
Draft Loaded	4'5"
Weighed	Killaloe 1937
Engine	Bolinder E Type 15Hp
Home Base	Lough Ree

worked on her for a time. Johnny and Mick Donoghue and Anthony Kennedy were in 75M around 1948. She was tied up then for some time as her engine bed needed to be replaced.

When the canal closed down in December 1959, 75M was one of the 14 boats that were taken back for six months to bring Guinness to Limerick and help in the de-commissioning of the Company

Courtesy — Shorthall Collection

Heritage Boat 76M

The Grand Canal's fate as a transport route was sealed in November 1959 with the announcement from CIE of its withdrawal from trading. According to canal records 76M was the last cargo boat to leave Edenderry Harbour. In January 1960 she was one of the 14 boats brought back for

57M, 76M & 72M at James's St. harbour (Guinness)

James's St. Harbour. The barges for sale were 31M, 44M, 66M, 67M, 70M, and 76M. It is not known who bought the boat or if indeed it was sold at that time but she was purchased as a raw hull in the early 1980's by Captain Jack Bagnall an Aer Lingus pilot. Over the following 14 years Jack very carefully converted her. She was bought by the Baker-Kenny family in 1997 and is one of the most familiar boats on the waterways as it is regularly seen on the Canal, Shannon and Erne systems.

Crew Included—

Around 1940 Henry Doyle (Allenwood), who was working on 76M, lost his leg in an accident when it got caught in a rope at the stores in Athy. In the early 1940's the Barge was worked by the Cross-Family from Robertstown. Tom Bowers started work

76M arriving in Carlow – 2005

six months to work on the canal to help in the closing down of the CIE canal Depots and to bring porter to Limerick. Her crew for that period were Tommy Hannon (Garrykennedy/Banagher) as the Skipper, Mick "Oil Hat" Connolly (Allenwood) was Driver/Engineman and Johnny Conroy (Robertstown) was Deckhand.

On September 29th 1965 a Sale of Canal Barges by Public Auction took place at

Photo – Brendan Davis

on 76M in 1943, working alongside Tom, Paddy and Tosh Cross from Ballyteague. Jack Connolly from Derrymullen also worked on her around then before he left to go and work on 66M. Jim Bolger from Graiguenamagh, his father "Lawlor" Bolger and his uncle Seamus Bolger and Robert Bolger also worked on 76M as did Joe Connolly Shannon Harbour and Tommy Hannon.

Technical Details	
Reg. No.	76M
Built By	Vickers (Ireland) Ltd
Year	1937
Construction	Riveted Steel
Length	61' 6"
Beam	13' 1.5"
Payload	61 Tons
Draft	4' 5"
Weighed	Killaloe 1937
Engine	Bolinder E Type 15Hp
	120hp Ford D Series 6 Cyl
Home Base	Jamestown

Retired boats prior to auction—1960   Courtesy — Shorthall Collection

Heritage Boat 77M

77M was built in 1937 by the Ringsend Dockyard Company otherwise known as a McMillan boat. Together with 78M & 79M she was built 18" longer and 3" wider than the standard M boat so she measured 61ft 6" x 13ft 3". In the early 1950's Eddie Cummins from Edenderry worked with Paddy Aungier on this boat. Poor old Eddie had a sad ending when he drowned off 77M in Daingean in 1954/55. It happened while loading beet around Christmas time. That wasn't the only tragedy connected on 77M as George Fitzpatrick from Dublin drowned off her below Portumna while towing a row boat for a man from Garrykennedy. The row boat was being towed up the lake behind the barge, coming up the lake George pulled the boat up to the barge and got into it. After a while he decided to go back to the barge so he went to the front of the row boat and pulled on the tow rope. The combination of his weight and the pull on the rope pulled down the nose of the boat and he fell in the lake. His body was picked up by another boat the following day. At another time Robert Mahon was skipper with Paddy Mahon and Paddy Delaney. Her last crew were all from Banagher, Andy Maloney was in charge (Skipper), Tom

'Thick' Donnelan was the Driver/Engineman and Will 'Abie' Maloney was Deckhand.

77M in 2005—Andy Maloney on board

77M wasn't sold off by CIE but was converted to a dredger. Her bow was cut down to the waterline and a Priestman dredger fitted. Her Bolinder engine was replaced with a 59hp air cooled Lister diesel engine. Tommy Doyle and Christy Daly were her first crew, John Doherty , John Whelan Graiguenamagh and Joe Logan also worked on her. In 1986-87 Kit Moran and Ger Nolan was the crew on 77M when she worked on the Circular Line in Dublin. She moved to the Barrow around 1995-96 and was retired from service in 1997.

She still belonging to Waterways Ireland and is currently lying in the canal outside the WI Maintenance depot at Fenniscourt Lock.

James's Street Harbour

Heritage Boat 78M

78M was built as part of the new Grand Canal Company's motorised fleet in 1939 by Ringsend Dockyard Company. Ringsend boats were fondly remembered as McMillen boats after the builder and were allegedly faster and lighter to handle, than Vickers boats. Like

the other boats in the new fleet she was powered by a 15hp Bolinder semi diesel and capable of carrying over 50 ton payload.

In 1946 Jim Gill joined the boat to work with his father Paddy, who was the Skipper, and brother Tom, the engineman. Tragedy

struck in 1948 when 78M hit Hartley bridge, in Ticknevin, and Jim's father was knocked into the canal by the tiller and drowned. Jim stayed with boat until 1949.

"Paddy Gill Junior. . . decided to trade 31M for 78M because of his father's connection with 78M. He managed to close the deal with the addition of a few pounds and became the proud owner of 78M"

78M wasn't sold of in 1960 but stayed with CIE and was used intermittently as a maintenance boat until the 1970's when it was retired. Paddy Gill Jnr. had bought the 31M from CIE at Auction in 1965, but on hearing that 78M was potentially on the market, decided to trade 31M for 78M because of his father's connection with 78M. He managed to close the deal with the addition of a few pounds and became the proud owner of 78M.

Paddy brought 78M to Graignamanagh where he has kept the original Bolinder

78M—2005

and fitted out the hold for accommodation. While Paddy doesn't live locally, his brother Jim looks after the boat and the Bolinder is regularly started. 78M has been known to venture up to Bagnelstown to the festival and will hopefully be a regular attendee.

Crew Included—
1943 to Late 40's...
Paddy Kennedy (Skipper), Joe Connolly, Shannon Harbour, (Engineman &

Skipper Tpy), "Hairy" Loonan, (Deckman ,Engineman Tpy), Billy Murphy (Greaser), Pee Judge, (Greaser & Deckman Tpy), Jack O'Neill (Greaser Tpy)

1949 to 1954...
Tom Lawlor, (Deckman), Jack Betson (Deckman), Paddy Cross (Deckman), "Ninety" Blythe (Deckman & Engineman Tpy), Christy Blythe (Deckman & Engineman).

The James's Street Harbour   Copyright, GUINNESS Archive, Diageo, Ireland

Heritage Boat 79M

79M was the last boat built for the Grand Canal Company and went into service in 1939. She was built to maximum dimensions for locks on the canal and measured 61ft 9″ x 13ft 3″.

day to load the boat with shovels and wheel barrows. The next day was to get back to where they were working and the third day was to unload the load of clay. It was unloaded on to the bank with shovels. She still had a Bollinder engine fitted during that time.

79M in Banagher

In the early 1980's the maintenance department got Jackie Thomas to put a hydraulic crane on her bow and they also re-engined her. Frank Dowdle and his son Michael worked on after that. In the 1980's after Board of Work's took over the running of the canal there was a lot of dredging work done especially around

79M wasn't sold off by CIE but worked from 1960 to around 1980 as a maintenance 'Muck' boat on the Canal. Her crew during the 1970's were Paddy Nolan, Willy Flynn and Mick Gurry. After them Willy Flynn, Johnny Dunne and Joe Cornly worked on her until she was eventually taken out of service as a Clay boat circ 1980.

Dublin. At that time three dredgers were working in Dublin 79M, 32E and 77M. When the Dublin job was finished 79M continued to be used for dredging on the canal before being retired in the 1990's.

79M is currently lying disused in Waterways Ireland's maintenance yard in Tullamore.

The schedule for the Muck Boats (also referred to as Clay Boats or Gravel Boats) was one day travelling to Cock Bridge one

Crew included—
In the late 1950's Tom Connolly, Paddy Nolan and Tom Bowers worked on her.

John Connolly and Andy Shorthall

Banagher Jack (Carroll), Tom and Larry Finnegan as well as Jim Gill also worked on her at one time or another. John Connolly (Graiguenamagh) finished up on 79M in 1960 and at the young age of 24 he was pensioned off by CIE at £1-2-10 a week.

When the canal closed down in December 1959, 79M was one of the 14 boats that were taken back for six months to bring Guinness to Limerick and help in the de-commissioning of the company stations. Its crew for the time were Tom Bowers (Robertstown/Killaloe) was Skipper, Bert Conroy (Robertstown/Killaloe) was Driver/Engineman.

Heritage Boat 4B

4B was built in Portadown for the Leinster Carbonising Turf Co. and was first weighed at Killaloe in August 1912, and again in 1939. She was later transferred to the new Turf Development Board before been passed on to Mr. James Doyle of Allenwood, who had a mooring just west of the Skew Bridge. The barge was designed as an early motor vessel fitted and fitted with a Bolinder 12hp single cylinder engine.

During the "Emergency" (1939-45) James Doyle carried turf from the midlands into Dublin. After the war she was sold on to Jack Gill who then owned 31B. Jack is remembered for carrying large bales of cotton to the Shannon on the deck of 4B. These bales were 8'x4' and being a hack boat they were piled high on the boat so the tiller man had to nearly jump up and down to see where he was going (especially when he met another boat). The height of the chimney had to be extended with a broomstick to align the boat with the bridges.

In the fifties it was owned by a local publican Jack O'Neill who used it to carry

> *"Legend has it he never had to jump because he was thrown ashore by the force of the boat hitting the wall"*

timber. Records confirm that 4B made numerous trips on the lower Barrow between 1951 and 1953 mostly with round timber wharfage. These were through St. Mullins, Graiguenamagh, Ballykeenan, Graiguenamagh, and Inistioge. Jack O'Neill operated as a skipper/owner and had a deckhand called Leary who was always told to jump off the boat with the stop rope when they reached the quay. Legend has it he never had to jump because he was thrown ashore by the force of the boat hitting the wall.

Later 4B left the canal system for the Suir where she was used by Mr. John Power to draw washed building sand from the river bed at Mooncoin. It was here that she was spotted and bought by Mr. Ian Johnston, in 1972, who brought her to the Shannon.

4B was originally fitted with a Bolinder engine. It was modernised with a 55Hp diesel engine taken from a Thames Trader lorry, complete from radiator to

May 2000

gearbox. The gearbox and propeller shaft were coupled using the original lorry prop shaft and universal joints which allowed the flexibility in positioning the engine off centre and forward. Whilst being moored near Dromineer she was gradually converted, including the addition of a coach house roof and wheelhouse, and used as a holiday barge on the Shannon until purchased by Stephen Gentleman in 2001 and brought back to the canal system in order to carry out further conversion work.

Her hull remains in excellent condition and she is currently moored at Hazelhatch undergoing fitting out as a live-a-board.

A barge 'convoy' leaving James's Street Harbour　　　　　　　Courtesy—Shortall Collection

The Williams & Woods
Heritage Boat 31 B
also known as "The Jam Boat"

Built in Northern Ireland, circa 1910, for D. E. Williams Ltd. of Tullamore. She was weighed in Killaloe in 1912 and traded, carrying grain, on the Barrow till 1927. From 1927 till 1946 she traded on the Grand Canal under two owners, P. Cafferky of Mountmellick and J. Gill. In 1946 she transferred to Williams & Woods Ltd, for whom she's still named, and carried various confectioneries the length and breadth of the navigation, a welcome relief from wartime rationing. In 1958 she was taken over by CIE and her engine was removed.

Sold to a civil engineering Company, she was used, alongside the "Eclispe Flower", a former Ranks Flour Co. barge, as a floating platform for a crane during the building of the new bridge in Wexford in 1959. She then lay abandoned, either under the bridge or in the salt marshes beside it until 1978. At this point her purchase was negotiated and she was refloated by Pat Benson who, having fitted a BMC engine, brought her up the coast to Dublin and on to Athlone. Her last act as a working boat appears to have been in 1979 when she was used to carry building supplies to one of the islands on Lough Ree for the construction of a house. She was then brought to Edenderry, where she was converted. She was sold again in the early nineties to a Mr Ward, but fell into bad repair, was vandalised and sank in Shannon Harbour around 1997. Bought by Michael and Mai Devlin in 2000, she was refloated and following a spell in Shannon Harbour drydock, was brought north, to Co. Leitrim where she underwent a refit. Over

the winter of 2001/2, a Perkins 6354.4 engine was fitted to replace the BMC engine which had "expired" on the way back from the Lough Derg Rally. Hydraulic steering was fitted during the winter of 2002/3. I bought her from Mick and Mai in October 2004 and, following some hull plating and construction of a superstructure over the bow cabin in Roosky dry-dock, took possession in March 2005.

Although she has hydraulic steering fitted, her tiller is still attached. Mick Devlin told me he was "loathe to cut it off", and I must admit, the thought of cutting it off now, after 95 years of faithful service, doesn't appeal to me either. 2005 , travelling as part of the HBA fleet, saw her back on the Barrow, participating in various events along the navigation and visits, on tidal waters, to New Ross, Inistioque, Carrick-On-Suir and to Waterford (for the Tall Ships Event)—must have reminded her of her days in Wexford Harbour!

A hack boat on the Circular Line. (Coras Iompair Eireann).

Technical Details

Reg. No.	31B
Type	"B" (Bye-Trader or Hack Boat)
Name	The Williams and Woods
Built by	Either Portadown Foundry or Bright Patent Pulley Co. Lisburn
Built for	D. E.Williams, Tullamore
Length	60 feet
Beam	12ft 9in.
Draft	3 feet
Material	Riveted steel
Ballast	Concrete - 14 Tonnes
Engines	Bolinder, 1919-1958
	BMC 1978 - 2001
	Perkins 6354.4 2002 to date
	She also had twin Seagull outboards attached to the rudder in 1978 or 1979

31B in Waterford—2005

Brendan Davis

The Heritage Boat Association attend a number of events on the waterways each year to enable people to see the boats and to learn some of their history. One such event in 2005 was the Tall Ships Race which started from Waterford. 31B, in the photo at the top of the page, and a number of other former trading boats attended to enable visitor to also see a very different type of boat. Some of these are pictured above.

Brendan Davis

Heritage Boat 34 B

Canal Boat 34 B was built in Shannon Harbour in 1896. She was owned by Shackeltons Mills at Milford Co Carlow. This mill was run by Ebenezer Shackelton a relative of the great explorer. In 1913 she was owned by Moores of Carlow. She was weighed at Killaloe for the Moores on the 8th Sept 1928. She was used by the Moore family to carry general cargo on the Barrow and Grand Canal until trade declined on the system. She is also reputed to have been used for icebreaking on the canal and this was confirmed by an old canal man who claimed that he saw her

Mespil Road, Dublin—2001

Courtesy—Shortall Collection

in action in this role at Ticknevin being towed by a number of horses. During the Second World War turf was purchased in the Ticknevin area and taken to Dublin. On a trip through the lock at Ticknevin an elderly local man on seeing the boat in the lock made the statement to me "You know 34B put food on many a table in this area during the war." 34B is reputed to have been shot at during the Easter rising in 1916 while leaving Ringsend

basin. There is indeed what appears to be a bullet hole visible inside the hull in the engine room on the port side. The Moore family owned 34B until trade ceased on the system in 1959. From the decline in trade in the early 50's she had remained tied up at Graigcullen, home port of the Moore's. She was later purchased by Jim Dillon who carried out the first conversion on her. The late David Wheeler later purchased her in a derelict state at Rathangan and he was responsible for the present conversion.

34 B carrying a load of wheat moored at Sallins June 1939

She was later owned by a syndicate of German nationals along with the late Des Barry. She was purchased in 1990 by Gerry

& Geraldine Gavin who made significant changes to the interior. The many plaques on display inside testify to the many rallies she has participated in since she came to the Shannon.

"vandals cut her loose from the Apparel jetty and she went over the weir"

In the late 80's she had the dubious distinction of passing through Athlone without using the lock. On that occasion vandals cut her loose from the Apparel jetty and she went over the weir. There are many stories around Athlone of adventures aboard 34 B involving previous owners.

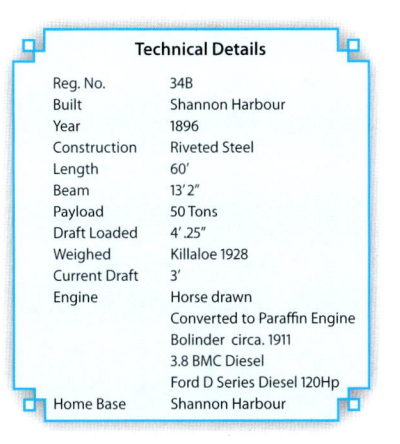

Technical Details

Reg. No.	34B
Built	Shannon Harbour
Year	1896
Construction	Riveted Steel
Length	60'
Beam	13'2"
Payload	50 Tons
Draft Loaded	4'.25"
Weighed	Killaloe 1928
Current Draft	3'
Engine	Horse drawn
	Converted to Paraffin Engine
	Bolinder circa. 1911
	3.8 BMC Diesel
	Ford D Series Diesel 120Hp
Home Base	Shannon Harbour

Courtesy—Shortall Collection

The Snark
Heritage Boat 42B

42B was built in Portadown in 1913 for P & H. Egan Ltd., Tullamore who had her weighed in Killaloe in 1913. She was used as a general cargo boat doing a scheduled run to and from Dublin every week. A typical weekly timetable would have entailed leaving Tullamore early Monday morning to arriving in Dublin Wednesday morning. The crew would have to unload the boat of up to 50 ton of cargo and reload her before departure Wednesday evening. Typical cargos to Dublin included malt, whiskey, grain, with general cargo and Guinness on the back load. Back to Tullamore by Saturday where she would be unloaded and reloaded ready for the next run on Monday morning.

With the decline of canal traffic Egan's sold her on to S. McKenzie in Dublin. She was subsequently converted in the early 1960's by a CIE engineer called Costello who also fitted a 1940's six cylinder Leyland diesel engine together with a Commer gearbox of similar vintage.

She changed hands a number of times in the following years but some of the owners included members of the Loraine Cycling Club, Dublin, Dr. McGarry, who sold her on to a Mr. O'Reardon of Athlone in 1974. Joe McCoole and his wife Joan have had her since 1981

The interior layout has been changed very little since the 1970's, but everything above deck has been replaced in steel.

It was fitted with a hydraulic steering, replacing the wire rope one in 1999. The bow was re-plated in 2001 and the bilges are currently been addressed in Shannon Harbour.

"Snark" was based in Athlone for years, spent some time in the 1980's in Hazelhatch but is now based in Shannon Harbour. It is used as a family boat cruising the Shannon and the Erne and with a family of six kids she gets a lot of use all year round.

Snark approaches Quivvy—2003

HBA boats in Banagher—2006

Heritage Boat 95B

Canal Boat 95B commenced life transporting malt for the Barrow Transport Company from Minch Nortons in Athy to the Guinness Brewery in Dublin. It passed into the ownership of Tom Hughes in Athy in 1956, used for mixed cargo including carrying sugar beet to the factory in Carlow. At the closure of the canal in 1960 Tom Hughes continued to trade with his barges and 95B was the last boat to carry beet into Carlow Sugar Company in 1962.

After the canal closure, 95B found its way into the ownership of a construction company where it was used as a floating raft for the construction of the new bridge in Youghal. On the completion of the bridge, she was auctioned and purchased by Eugene Suffin, of Waterford, who intended to use her for sand dredging on the river Suir. This was not bargined for by 95B and shortly after it was sold, it broke its mooring in a gale and foundered against the rocks at the base of the bridge it had

Sunk (low tide) in Youghal

On the Barrow 2005

helped to build. Several efforts were made to repair the damage without success. 95B lay in that position for some years until finally drawing the attention of Cork and Waterford Co. Councils who agreed that's she was a hazard to navigation and an ugly sight but disputed who was responsible for her removal. An appreciable file built up in Transport house in Dublin regarding the vessel

In May 1967 the nose of 95B was spotted by George Spears sticking out of the water under the bridge in Youghal. After waiting for the tide to turn she exposed itself covered with all kinds of marine life. Enquiries were made and the vessel purchased for the pricely sum of £25 less one for luck however a further £21 had to be paid to Youghal Harbour Commissioners for damage to the bridge. George mobilised a team from Athy who spent many weekends in July 1967 removing seaweed, limpets, shell fish, and silt. When the hull was finally exposed, the gashes that were evident, were repaired in situ, allow her to be floated on an incoming tide at 2.30am.

Further repairs were carried out in Youghal Harbour until she was declared fit for the 70 mile tow by trawler to New Ross in June 1968. A further tow by a canal work boat delivered her to the "Steamers Pool" from where she traveled the remaining journey to St. Mullin's by sail improvised with the aid of a sheet of clear polythene. The 40 mile journey to Athy was an even greater challenge as the canals had been overgrown by weed in 1968 and it proved impossible to tow by horse or boat. Eventually with the aid of a winch and several hundred feet of rope 95B was dragged home to Athy.

The first conversion of 95B was started immediately by George on arrival in Athy in 1969 where over a 3 year period she had a Bolinder reinstalled, which was bought with accessories from a Mr. O. Keifer in Mooncoin, for £18.

She eventually became a comfortable boat attending all rallies throughout the Shannon and had the privilege of having her own harbour in Terryglass. In 1986 George treated 95B to a new Perkins 6354 diesel engine and gearbox. Unfortunately George passed away in 1987 which was a big loss to those that who him.

I had spotted 95B in Terryglass several times and always admired her fine boat lines and so in 1998 we succeeded in purchasing her and brought up the canal to Edenderry where she is undergoing the current refit as a family boat. A new superstructure, decks, and underwater plating has been completed. An extensive internal fit out is to follow.

95B has experienced fame and notoriety, having been driven by Bishop (Later Cardinal) Daly in 1976, appeared in National Geographic 1976 and visited by a President of Ireland, Patrick Hillery in 1983. In 2005 still only partly converted she travelled

Re-Paint—Shannon Harbour 1973

down the Barrow to the Tall Ships event in Waterford picking up the last bag of sugar from Carlow Sugar Company along the way.

95B has always had a reputation as a hospitable boat where craic and music were abundant and we hope that she will carry on in this tradition and bring as much enjoyment as she gave the previous owners.

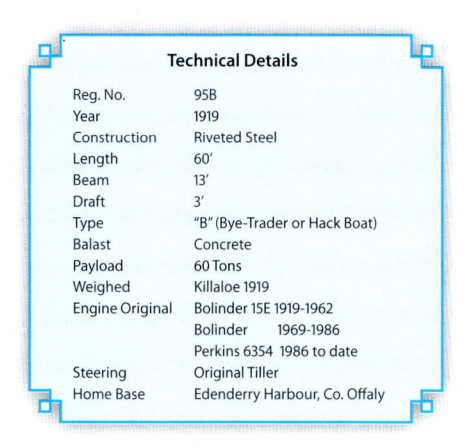

Technical Details

Reg. No.	95B
Year	1919
Construction	Riveted Steel
Length	60'
Beam	13'
Draft	3'
Type	"B" (Bye-Trader or Hack Boat)
Balast	Concrete
Payload	60 Tons
Weighed	Killaloe 1919
Engine Original	Bolinder 15E 1919-1962
	Bolinder 1969-1986
	Perkins 6354 1986 to date
Steering	Original Tiller
Home Base	Edenderry Harbour, Co. Offaly

Snipe
Heritage Boat 103B

103B was built in 1928 for the Grand Canal Company but the order was cancelled and it was sold to Thomas McDermott of Ticknevin in 1930. 103B is one of two modern built M style hulls that didn't go to the GCC but went straight into private ownership, the other being 118B. Even though she was built to take an engine she was operated for the first two years without one so was towed by a horse. The Bolinder was installed in 1932. 103B was a private cargo boat on the canal, privately owned or operated boats were called Hack Boats or Bye Traders. She operated on the Grand Canal and the Barrow. Mrs McDermott told a Ruth Casey in 1975 that 103B did one trip to Limerick.

The canal closed down to commercial traffic in 1959 but most of the private boats were tied up earlier in the 1950's. Its not know for sure what happened her next but it's believed that she went to Dundalk Harbour Commissioners. In April 1975 a P. Taylor sold it to Alan Algeo. Alan sold it on that September to Mick Webb and Ruth Casey. It was just a hull at that stage and was sunk on a sand bank but with the help of a few friends they raised her and towed her to Athlone. Ruth and Mick converted her and instead of (like everybody else at the time) using wood and mineral felt to cover the cargo hold they used cement with chicken wire through it. She was christened Snipe and

has spent most of it time since then under the railway bridge in Athlone. One reason was that Mike and Ruth were living on it but over the years the second reason took over in that the engine had seized up. Mike and Ruth went boating further afield and sold 103B to Jim Reddy in September 2001. Jim got her towed down to Shannon Harbour in 2005 where he got some hull work done. She was towed back to Athlone and plans are currently afoot to get her moving under her own power in the not too distant future.

As an aside, Jim is a well known pallette knife painter, and teaches regularly in Athlone College. His paintings of river scenes and indeed individual barges are well known, so if you are passing through Athlone, or would like a painting of your barge or boat give him a call.

Snipe in Athlone—2004

Clerical staff loding boats during strike of 1911

Copyright, GUINNESS Archive, Diageo, Ireland

Emily
Heritage Boat 107B

107B was weighed in Killaloe on 21st January 1930. She is believed to have been built in Ringsend a short time previous to this. This makes her at least 76 years old. She was operated by Michael Fennell who traded between Carlow and Dublin carrying general goods. She was subsequently owned by a Mr. Power from Carrick on Suir who in turn sold her on to Roadstone. She left the canal navigation on 7th March 1955 for the river Suir to engage in the dredging of sand from the river.

By 1969 107B had disappeared from sight, and was long forgotten, when an advertisement appeared in the Irish Press advertising two canal boats for sale. At this time Robertstown on the Grand Canal was experiencing a rebirth led by local priest Father P. J. Murphy who persuaded the local committee to invest in the boats with a view to running boat excursions on the canal.

The two boats, identified as 107B & 52M, were inspected on the Suir at Mooncoin where 107B was found afloat with 52M sunk nearby. Both boats were purchased. £700 was paid to Roadstone for 107B.

In July 1969 a group from Robertstown assembled at Mooncoin to take charge of the recovery operation of the two boats. The 52M was in very poor condition and presented a huge challenge to the men from Robertstown which they overcame using some novel innovations.

With the boat afloat both boats were towed to St Mullins to have further repairs carried out. A BMC truck engine was purchased and with its original gearbox was installed into 107B. After several months of hard work both boats were ready to start the long journey to Robertstown. The plan was for 107B to tow 52M. This proved more difficult than anticipated and a tractor was used to tow the barges through the more difficult sections with it being carried on the deck of 107B when not needed. Other difficulties that impeded progress were the condition of Locks that were either leaking or silted up. Hay was used to seal locks and silt was flushed out of the locks to clear the passage for the boats.

"In July 1971 Mrs Barbara Castle, a member of the British Government, launched the 107B re-naming her the Emily"

At Borris Lock a large sandbank blocked the navigation. This was dug clear by the men from Robertstown who stripped off and, wearing old boiler suits, dug a channel in the riverbed to get the boats through. Finally the journey to Robertstown was completed and in winter 1970 work began in earnest on conversion of 107B into a passenger carrying vessel. John Tyrell of Arklow designed a superstructure that would accommodate 60 to 70 people.

In July 1971 Mrs Barbara Castle, a member

of the British Government, launched the 107B re-naming her the Emily. For a decade the "Emily" successfully carried dignitaries locals and tourists on trips along the GrandCanal. However by 1980 the glory days had passed and Emily was lying moored up and eventually became severely damaged by fire. In 1987 ownership of the Emily (107B) passed to DERTO (Dublin Eastern Regional Tourist Organisation) and on to MERTO (Midland and Eastern Regional Tourist Organisation) in 1992.

107B en route to Shannon Harbour (note the powerful engine)

In 2004 MERTO subsequently offered the 107B to a group of canal enthusiasts attached to Offaly Branch IWAI for restoration on condition that the Emily (107B) would be used to promote the Grand Canal throughout the inland navigations of Ireland. Out of this was born the "107B project group".

The group has put in place an extensive plan to restore the boat and develop it into an exhibition centre/museum which would attend festivals and rallies on the waterways promoting the grand canal in all its facets. It would also be made available to schools and educational groups as a facility to teach young people about the Grand Canal.

November 2004 saw the move of 107B to Tullamore for survey and inspection. A small cruiser was used to push the boat some of the way and a 15Hp outboard fitted to the tiller took over for the remainder of the journey.

"the group demonstrate great skill in begging, cajoling and using all their powers of persuasion to get help on board"

In dry dock, when the extent of the works became clear, the project was moved to Shannon Harbour dry docks to begin work on the hull. This work commenced in late February 2006 with volunteers assembled from as far away as Antrim and Enniskillen. People within the group demonstrate great skill in begging, cajoling and using all their powers of persuasion to get help on board. Steel arrived from Northern Ireland along with welders who gave their services free. Volunteers spent long days cleaning the hull, preparing steel, rust removal, painting and welding to make the hull watertight.

On Sunday the 2nd April 2006 the original boat number 107B was painted onto the bow of the boat and she was again canal boat 107B.

Much work remains to be done.

Technical Details	
Reg. No.	107B
Built	Ringsend Dock Yard
Year	1930'S
Construction	Riveted Steel
Length	62'
Beam	13' 4"
Payload	54 Tons
Draft Loaded	4' 3"
Weighed	Killaloe 1936
Current Draft	3'
Home Base	Shannon Harbour

Bowler
Heritage Boat 108 B

*T*he barge was built in 1898 as a horse-drawn boat, the No. 17 by the Passage Dock Company. Fifteen years later, in 1913, a Bolinder engine was fitted—two years after the first of these engines were fitted to barges—it was re-numbered the 17M.

In about 1930 the barge was bought by Patrick Nolan, a boatman from Rathangan who had previously owned the 80B. The barge was again re-numbered as a hack boat, the 108B. Patrick was well known up and down the Grand Canal System as the 'Bowler Nowlan' as he characteristically wore a bowler hat. It was from him that the barge derived its name, the Bowler.

In the early 1950's, following the transfer

"Patrick Nolan moved up to the 9th Lock at Clondalkin and, with the 108B tied up to the bank, opened a general store which became a popular stop for boatmen"

of the Grand Canal Company to CIE, work for the private boatman became slack so Patrick Nolan moved up to the 9th Lock at Clondalkin and, with the 108B tied up to the bank, opened a general store which became a popular stop for boatmen. Sometime in the middle to late 1950's, Patrick Nolan sold the barge to CIE. The engine was removed and the stern gland was filled with concrete. The barge was then used as a gravel boat in the Engineering Department and was re-numbered to 94E. The barge ended its working days at the 12th Lock where it lay half submerged for a good many years. At that time it had wooden decks throughout and a companionway across the middle of the hold. There were no engine room or bow cabin housings; these were entered through open hatches in the deck. The barge was of standard length but it was well known that it was marginally beamier than other barges at the stern. On occasion, the barge got stuck in lock gates. It was essential that for those locks which were slightly narrower, the lock gates had to be completely open before

the barge could enter the chamber.

In December 1970, it was auctioned by Morrisseys Auctioneers on behalf of CIE. The barge was bought at this auction by five university students; it was refloated and towed by car into Dublin with the intention

engines strapped to the rudder, on to the 13th Lock. The Bowler remained there until 1979 when she was towed by rowing boat with outboard by Paddy and Anne Wilkinson to Athy, a trip that took seven days to complete. A Coventry Climax 36HP marine engine was installed. Finally under

of dry-docking at the Grand Canal Harbour, James's Street. Unfortunately the basin and dry dock were closed while on passage so the barge ended up on at Wilton Place on the 'Ring' where the initial first conversion began. Following objections by local residents because of noise from angle grinders and welders, the barge was moved on to the Herbert Place section where work continued for a further 12 months.

"Patrick was well known up and down the Grand Canal System as the 'Bowler Nowlan' as he characteristically wore a bowler hat"

The barge, now known as the 'Bowler' and reverting to the 108B, was towed back to the 12th Lock by car and tractor lorry and, with the assistance of two out-board

her own 'steam' she was taken down the Barrow to Fenniscourt Lock where she was completely stripped and the superstructure built in its present form, with retention of the original tiller, by Paddy Wilkinson. Paddy formerly owned the 76M.

In the late 1980's the Bowler was taken to Dromineer on Lough Derg where she provided sleeping accommodation for a sailing school. In 1991 the hull was completed replated and since then the Bowler has been based at Shannon Harbour. She has undergone a number of internal and structural modifications with the assistance Paul Doran and Jean Colvin of the MV Liverpool, including the installation of a new 78HP Nissan marine engine. Of the original five students just one remains; for the last 30 years the Bowler has been owned by Philip and Vivienne Mayne and, since their return to Ireland, it operates principally between Lough Ree and Lough Derg.

Terrapin
Heritage Boat 112B

She was built in 1873 at Poratdown Foundry as a horse drawn boat. She worked on the Royal and had Royal number 21 and was known as "Black Swan". Its not known how she ended up on the Royal as she is a 60ft boat and Royal Canal boats were 70ft. In the 1920's she was sold off to John Roche and began trading on

the Grand Canal as 112B. He sold it on to M. Dowling in Dublin. Denis Lynch of Garrykennedy bought her in June 1949 for the sum of £40 including the horse. Denis sometime later positioned her on the cill of Meelick Lock and had her stern cut out to take a stern tube and propeller shaft. A Bolinder engine was then fitted. She was then used as a Hack Boat on the Shannon carrying various cargos such as Slate from the quarries in Portroe, Turf during the summer and Corn in the harvest.

In 1961 Ken Simmons purchased her and lived aboard with his family, after conversion until the early 1990's. Ken was suffering from failing health at that time so he became a land lubber so the Terrapin fell into disrepair. Ken sold her in 1996. As she had no working engine and she was based in Killaloe he towed her for the new owner to Tuamgraney. Enthusiasm got the better of the new owner who stripped her out finding as he went along, the more he ripped the further he had to go. Eventually he ended up with a bare hull. During the winter of 1998, the Terrapin sank in Tuamgraney. The following Summer, as she was a hazard to navigation, she was removed by Duchas (now Waterways Ireland) and brought to their Portumna depot. It was from there that Martin and Mary O'Rourke the current owners bought her a few years later. They took her by road to Tullamore and have her on display beside the Round Lock House (loch 26) which they also own.

Fox
Heritage Boat 113 B

Built in 1937 by William McMullen (Ringsend Dockyard Company) in 1937. It was sold to Thomas Hughes of Athy and is stated to have cost 1,175 pounds. It worked on the Barrow line of the Grand Canal carrying mixed cargo. It was bought by the O.P.W. to be used as a maintenance boat on the Shannon in the early 1950's to replace the original Fox which Sid Shine had bought.

The Fox is one of Waterways Ireland's maintenance boats. It's basically a floating workshop. Its day to day operations are looking after routine maintenance of marker's, locks and bridge's on the upper Shannon. The boat and crew can also be involved in the building of new facilities and upgrades to existing ones. It's the oldest working vessel

still in operation in the Waterways fleet and has the charm of being a fantastic link to the past.

> *"It's the oldest working vessel still in operation in the Waterways fleet and has the charm of being a fantastic link to the past"*

Her crew in her early days (1950's) of doing maintenance was Dinny Madigan (Forman), his son Kevin and Jimmy O'Brien (Fitter/ Engineman), Mick Clifford (Portroe) and Paddy Lynch, from Garrykennedy—but

Courtesy—Shortall Collection

lived in Athlone, was the Skipper. When Dinny retired, Kevin took over as Foreman and later Michael McMahon (ex Lock Keeper in Limerick) joined the crew. In 1969 when the new purpose-built Shannon Maintenance boat the "Coill-an-Eo" was commissioned Kevin, Timmy, Mick and Michael joined her.

Paddy Lynch was left on the Fox and a fresh crew of Jimmy Conroy (Killaloe) and Tommy Ward (Athlone) joined him. Tony Hudson (the Lock Keeper in Roosky) worked on her for a while. In the late 70's, Paddy Lynch was still in charge with Anthony Donohue and Tony Hudson. After Tony went to take over the lock another former canal man—Tom Nolan of Killaloe—joined in his place. Tom Nolan left some time later and Andy Mangan from Daingean joined in his place. Pat got sick and Anthony took over as

skipper until he retired in the 1980's. Andy Mangan took over from him until he left. At that time George Herriott moved from the Coill-an-Eo to the Fox .

George is still the Skipper of the Fox with Faughna O'Regan, Tommy Carthy, Liam Sherringham and John Reddy. A nicer and friendlier bunch of lads you couldn't meet on the waterways.

34B Moored on the Barrow at Carlow

Heritage Boat 118 B

118 B

118B was the last motor canal boat built by the Ringsend Dockyard Company (McMillans) in 1939. She is of a similar design to those supplied to the Grand Canal Company but without the forward cabin roof which was often referred to as the top hat. With the onset of war there were no Bolinder engines available so W. P. & R. Odlums bought her and used her temporarily as a horse boat without the engine. The Grand Canal Company subsequently loaned them a Bolinder until they acquired one after the war.

This boat would have been numbered 80M if the Grand Canal Company had bought her for themselves and the canalmen often referred to her as such. Her maiden voyage was on the 29th of November 1939. During

> *"With the onset of war there were no Bolinder engines available so W. P. & R. Odlums bought her and used her temporarily as a horse boat without the engine"*

118B working   Courtesy—Shortall Collection

her period with Odlum's she was crewed, for almost all her working life, by Jim Kelly from Ballyteague with his son Dan and Johnny "The Rake" Connolly. With the closure of the canal traffic she was sold by Odlums in the 1950's and ended up in Waterford where she was used by the Harbour Commissioners for the maintenance of channel navigation markers in the river. A large bow roller was fitted to the front deck to accommodate the lifting and deployment of the large steel marker buoys.

The current owner purchased her in 2004 and immediately set about

118B awaiting restoration

removing the cumbersome bow roller on the foredeck. She was brought up the Barrow and the Grand Canal to Shannon Harbour where she is awaiting extensive refurbishment after years of loyal service in the salty waters of the Suir estuary.

Courtesy—Shortall Collection

The G-Boats
Heritage Boats

Most people will have seen ex-Grand Canal trading boats, now converted into spacious pleasure craft, and still making their way around the waterways system. The M-boats, formerly Grand Canal Company (GCC) motor boats, are most common, but B-boats survive too: they were owned by "bye-traders", independent individuals or companies, rather than by the GCC itself. E-boats were run by the GCC Engineering Department. Boats could change categories and sometimes GCC boats were hired out as hack boats, often to their own skippers.

But what about G-boats? Well, back in 1939, much of the world was engaged in a spot of bother that became known as the Second World War. Independent Ireland was officially neutral, but was affected by developments elsewhere. Accordingly, on 3 September 1939, the Oireachtas declared a state of emergency. Incidentally, it didn't get around to rescinding that state of emergency until 1976, when it declared another one instead. During the main part of The Emergency, 1939–1945, fuel was in short supply, so the government sought to have more turf brought to Dublin. As the canals conveniently pass through bogs, the government funded the construction of 29 wooden horse-drawn canal-boats, which were leased to various traders but were marked as G-boats. Matt Thompson remembers them—

Canal knowledge – by *Matt Thompson*
When the Second World War broke out in 1939, even though we were not directly involved, it had severe repercussions on Ireland: coal shortages affected almost everything. Railway services were cut down and in some cases branch lines were closed. The two canals running into Dublin were working flat out; everything that could float was brought into use including the E-boats, if they were available, drawing briquettes from Lullymore to Spencer Dock in Dublin.

My dear friends the Smullen family had a turf bank near Mount Street Bridge: people came from all over to buy. This family were working 28B and 7M; they also leased out 7G. It was great to see the canal so busy.

Big crowds gathered at Mellons Lock (Grand Canal St. Bridge) on the day 1G set out on its

maiden voyage to Turraun for its first load of machine-cut turf. To mark the occasion, the horses were put aside and GCC 36M was detailed to tow the new barge. The Irish Times had a splendid weekly issue called the Times Pictorial and the newspaper sent a reporter to travel with the crew to Co. Kildare to record this great event.

The working life of the G-boats was not very long, but during their time they played a very important part in the Emergency. Although the war ended in 1945 and the nation was slowly coming around to some kind of normality, the worst winter for years was to occur in 1947. The Grand and Royal Canals worked flat out to keep the city of Dublin from freezing: logs, turf (some very wet), briquettes and even sawdust were used.

After that, the G-boats became redundant. They could be found tied up or water-logged all over the system. One became a home for a gentleman and his dog at the mouth of the River Dodder at Ringsend: Mickey Blue told me he was very happy in his beautiful G-boat.

The last remaining bow & stern of a G-Boat on the shore of Lough Ree

Heritage Boat 4E

The Canal Boat which presently carries the number 4E, has a very interesting and varied history. It started working life as Horse Boat No. 53 on the Grand Canal and worked as such from 1896. In 1913 it had a Bolinder engine installed and became 23M. In 1935 it was sold without its engine to Joseph (Joe) Kane of Blackwood, Co. Kildare and became a Horse boat again with the number 111B. Joe Kane previously worked for Odlums Mills on their canal boats and was encouraged to go-it-alone so he bought 49B. The

> *He is said to have had a great attachment to her and when asked her number always replied, "three ones"*

following year he also bought 111B which he was to use the rest of his working life. He is said to have had a great attachment to her and when asked her number always replied, "three ones". The bent stem post known as the 'nose job' occurred when she was being towed by 41M into the inner basin in Ringsend with a cargo of 45 tons of wheat aboard. On approaching the lifting bridge, 41M slowed down and 111B veered out of control and into the bridge. The stem post and some bow plates were buckled forever. Joe sold 49B in 1937 and the following year he had an engine installed in 111B at a cost of £300. The main cargoes were turf into Dublin and wheat back

to Odlums at Sallins. Built of iron riveted construction with wooden decks, the only remnant of her horse-drawn days is part of the tow post about half way along the port side-inside the hull.

When Joe retired in 1952, 111B was acquired by C.I.E. and the last boat out of the Blackwood feeder before its closure. She was again relieved of her engine and brought to the Royal Canal by Engineering Section on maintenance duties and re-numbered 4E. While on the stretch between Ballynacarrigy and Abbeyshrule, a breach occurred on the bog section trapping 4E where she was finally abandoned in the dry canal. Her preservation was due to a former C.I.E. employee who had suffered a work accident, was allowed to live on her for some years. He was very liberal with the application of red lead and bitumen. In the early 70's, 4E was purchased

Trapped on the Royal Canal in 1970

by Robertstown Guild of Muintir Na Tire to add to its collection of canal boats. The salvage of 4E was not attempted and she remained settled at Ballynacarrigy. In October 1980 Joe Treacy purchased 4E where she lay for the sum of £1,800. He got it towed by tractor the half mile to a lock chamber, craned it onto a truck and brought her to Tullamore where it was re-floated on the Grand Canal. With the aid of a barge pole lent to him by John Weaving "as good as a spare engine", and powered again by 15 H.P. Evinrude outboard the trip to the 13th lock was completed over the two weekends in January 1981. Conversion to her present shape was completed by summer 1982.

On the Barrow—2005

"4E along with 35M, 68M and Dabu travelled from the Shannon to Dublin in 2001 in order to launch 'The Heritage Boat Association'. After a memorable trip the Minister Sile DeValera hoisted the H.B.A. Burgee on 4E's mast and a new era began"

At Tuamgraney on the Scarriff River she received and survived her second 'nose job' during the flooded 1986 Derg rally.

4E along with 35M, 68M and Dabu travelled from the Shannon to Dublin in 2001 in order to launch 'The Heritage Boat Association'. After a memorable trip the Minister Sile DeValera hoisted the H.B.A. Burgee on 4E's mast and a new era began.

Through a combination of age and her years of abandonment on the Royal Canal,

her feeble hull was in need of being completely re-plated, which was completed in 2002.

Over the last century 4E has come from horse boat to floating home-from-home with a lot of water under the keel. To those of you interested in a piece of canal history there is always a welcome aboard and anyone bitten with the dreaded 'Barge Fever' will never be put off by her skipper Joe Treacy as 4E has well repaid the blood, sweat and tears that has her still on the water today.

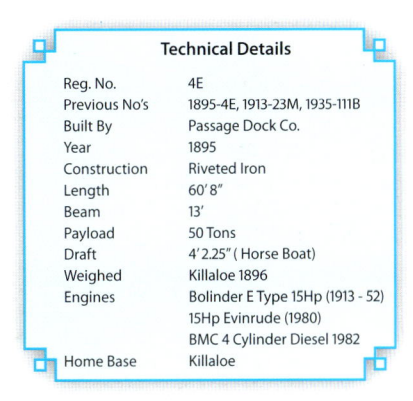

Technical Details	
Reg. No.	4E
Previous No's	1895-4E, 1913-23M, 1935-111B
Built By	Passage Dock Co.
Year	1895
Construction	Riveted Iron
Length	60' 8"
Beam	13'
Payload	50 Tons
Draft	4' 2.25" (Horse Boat)
Weighed	Killaloe 1896
Engines	Bolinder E Type 15Hp (1913 - 52)
	15Hp Evinrude (1980)
	BMC 4 Cylinder Diesel 1982
Home Base	Killaloe

Heritage Boat 32E

$32E$ was built as 32M by Ross & Walpole in 1926, for the Grand Canal Company, as a motorised general cargo boat capable of taking up to 50 Tons. The 15hp Bolinder installed was recovered from one of the original converted horse boats which had been decommissioned with the new fleet coming on stream. Like 31M it was a one-off prototype design that experimented

> *"...one time while being towed on the Barrow, the tug went through one arch in Goresbridge and 32M went through a different arch..."*

with a wedged shaped bow & stern and became known as the "Diamond" boat. Her hull profile caused difficulties with steering from the start, making her an unpopular boat amongst the boat crews. She "wouldn't go anywhere fast no matter what you did to her". "She was difficult to steer, one time while being towed on the Barrow, the Tug went through one arch in Goresbridge and 32M went through a different arch." Her design problems ensured that she was transferred to the Maintaince Department for other duties and became known as 32E. Here they cut the bow section down to the waterline to accommodate a Priestman Dredger which operated successfully for many years into the 1980's.

32E working   Courtesy—Shortall Collection

A "portacabin" was installed as crew accommodation in the hold which was covered over with steel to make it vandal proof.

32E has not been used as a dredger for quite some time and currently lies under water at the Waterways Ireland Maintenance Depot in Tullamore Harbour. The Priestman dredger has long since gone.

A boatman takes the tiller of 45M, adopts the stance, and takes a trip down memory 'canal'— taken at the boatmen's reunion, Banagher 2006,

Brendan Davis

The Enterprise
Heritage Boat 96E
also known as "The Floating Theatre"

T he Enterprise was operated as a motor boat numbered 98B by Patrick Farrell and was later sold in 1930 to Mrs. C. Farrell. It was the Farrells who named her the "Enterprise". 98B would have been known as a "Hack Boat" or a "Bye Trader" and was used as a general trading boat on the Canal. The CIE Maintenance Department bought 98B from the Farrell's on 27th January 1955 with the intention of

"In 1993 she was raised and filmed for the Late Late Show as part of their Antiques Special"

going into the maintenance department as a gravel boat. This didn't happen and she was instead put into general cargo duties and given the number 53M. (The previous boat numbered 53M was at the same time moved to Maintenance became 93E). From

talking to the boatmen they say that the reason that this happened was two fold. When CIE got 98B from the Farrell's she was in great condition as they always minded her and as the existing 53M was a small boat and an odd size somebody decided to swap them around and put the smaller boat into maintenance.

"In 1995 the Floating Theatre was launched by the then Minister for the Arts, Culture and Gaeltacht, Michael D. Higgins"

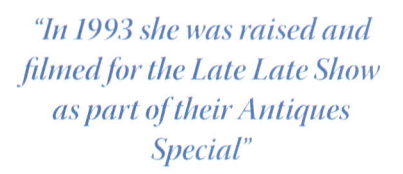

As 53M she was supposed to have been used to break the ice in Portarlington Harbour in 1955 as no other boats could move. As the traffic on the canal was dying down at that time it's not known if she worked after that. In 1959, she (53M) was transferred to the Canal Maintenance section and re-numbered 96E. Christy

Daly operated her as a gravel boat right up to 1973 when the Bolinder engine was removed and replaced with a Lister 29hp air cooled diesel engine. She continued in service until 1981. After that the engine was removed and she was left to eventually sink in the maintenance yard in Tullamore Harbour.

In 1993 she was raised and filmed for the Late Late Show as part of their Antiques Special. Following this and with the support of the Heritage Council, OPW, Board Failte and the Arts Council, the enterprise was converted to Ireland's first and only floating theatre.

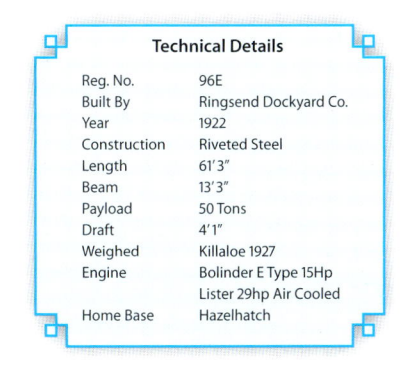

Technical Details	
Reg. No.	96E
Built By	Ringsend Dockyard Co.
Year	1922
Construction	Riveted Steel
Length	61'3"
Beam	13'3"
Payload	50 Tons
Draft	4'1"
Weighed	Killaloe 1927
Engine	Bolinder E Type 15Hp
	Lister 29hp Air Cooled
Home Base	Hazelhatch

tion of Conal Kearney the Enterprise began its series of Summer Schools for Children in 1997 and continues today during the summer months travelling the length and breadth of Irelands Inland Waterways.

> *"Under the direction of Conal Kearney the Enterprise began its series of Summer Schools for Children in 1997 and continues today..."*

Since its inception the Enterprise along with its faithful crew has entertained all who have come across her.

Crew Included—
Peter O'Farrell when she was 98B. One of her first crews with CIE was Tom McGrath with his sons Larry and Paddy. Then Pat Doyle and one of his sons took over. Andy and Abie Maloney with Tick Donnelan had her over the winter of 57-58.

Originally built of riveted steel with a wooden deck she was replated and re-decked with steel. Her interior was panelled with pitch pine and her true size can only be appreciated when you go down below decks. Her ownership transferred from the OPW to Conal Kearney and Derek Waters for the purpose of restoration and conversion to the floating Theatre.

In 1995 the Floating Theatre was launched by the then Minister for the Arts, Culture and Gaeltacht Michael D. Higgins. Under the direc-

Enterprise at Banagher in July 2006

Longford 53
Heritage Boat

How do you go about tracing the origins of an old canal boat? Let's see how we manage with this boat lying on the bank of the Royal Canal near Killeshin, Longford.

This barge, which can be seen on the left bank of the Royal Canal near Killeshin approaching Longford, has been reduced to a set of rusting ribs by the ravages of time. However, on closer examination you will notice the fine lines that are indicative of a horse boat from the 1890's. It was of mild steel construction on the lines of GCC Horse Boat 53 (4E), so it could well have been built by the Passage Dock Company in Cork. Maintenance boats on the Royal Canal were called Floats and were generally retired trade boats of various vintages and types.

A Hugh Hickey from Clondra reported some years ago that his uncle and a colleague worked on this barge at Killeshin when she was a maintenance boat commonly called a Float, as they were used as floating platforms. When the canal closed they were ordered to sink it where she was, at the junction of the Longford branch line off the Royal Canal.

> *"Is she too far gone to bring back? That's a matter of opinion, especially when one considers some of the rebuilding jobs that's been done on other barges over the past 20 years"*

It is possible to identify the number "53" painted on her hull which is the only reference we have to her past. Reviewing the indexes in Gerard Darcy's "Portrait of the Grand Canal", there were two no "53's" one became 25M which is now 4E and the other "53" became 4M. 4M was sold off and became a "Bye Trader" 123B in 1943. She was purchased back in 1945 and given the number 4M again. She was later moved to the Engineering Dept and re-numbered 86E. We don't know where 86E ended up, however from looking at old photo's of 4M we can identify close similarities that would suggest that Longford 53 and 4M/86E could be one and the same boat. This is further supported by the fact that a maintenance boat on the Grand Canal may have been transferred to the Royal Canal for works

Due to its original position in the Canal, it was in the way of Waterways Ireland's dredging programme. Ownership of the barge was transferred to Waterways Ireland who in turn managed to move the boat from the bottom of the canal to the side bank without distorting the original shape of the barge. Its lines are now as good as the day she was built.

Is she too far gone to bring back? That's a matter of opinion, especially when one considers some of the rebuilding jobs that's been done on other barges over the past 20 years. All that is needed is a person of vision with deep pockets and a determination to deliver her to her former glory.

The Killeshin barge is the only one of the five 'Float' series that is believed to have had a previous life as a motorised barge. However when it was working on the Royal it didn't have any engine and had to be pulled along by the men working on it.

G. C. C. Barge in lock

Rambler
Heritage Boat

The Rambler was one of five steamers purchased by the Midland Great Western Railway Company in 1875. The others were the Rattler, Mermaid, Conqueror and Pioneer. The MGWR had decided to enter the carrying business in 1871 and used horse-drawn boats at first. Three of the five steamers were small towing steamers and the other two were used to carry as well as tow. Because of her size the Rambler would have been one of the steamers used to carry. It is recorded that because of the size and weight of the steam engine, these boats could only carry up to 30 tons. The experiment was not a success and the company ceased to act as carriers in 1886.

Dr. V.S. Delany purchased the Rambler for his brother, T.W.Delany in 1923. She was in Ringsend Basin at the time and because she would not fit in the Grand Canal

locks he had to bring her down the Royal Canal, which took quite a long time as the canal was in poor condition. She had been converted by this time with a large saloon area and it is thought that she had been used as an inspection boat on the Royal. At Richmond Harbour they took out the steam engine and fitted a 60hp six-cylinder Glanefer paraffin engine, they completely re-decked her and restored the interior. T.W.Delany was a solicitor who lived in Longford and he kept the Rambler at Tarmonbarry in the summer and beside Richmond Harbour in the winter. He used her mostly for short trips but also attended the sailing regattas each year on the north Shannon and at the LRYC and LDYC. T.W.Delany owned her until his death in 1939 when she was sold to Captain Middleton, who brought her to Killaloe at the end of the second World War.

Tom Middleton and his wife, Ann, lived on board the Rambler at a mooring on the river, just above the ESB mill. They had plans to take in guests and to start a small sailing school based on the Rambler. This business never really took-off, although they did have a number of clients over the years. Eventually they built a house on the shore beside the boat, and moved in there. The Rambler was rarely moved in these years because of the difficulty in starting the Atlantic petrol/TVO six-cylinder engine. It required two strong men to swing the engine over. A small deck-house was built aft of the companionway in later years to act as a deck-saloon for guests. Eventually, in the late 1960s, they retired to Portugal and sold the Rambler.

"The Rambler was rarely moved in these years because of the difficulty in starting the Atlantic petrol/TVO six-cylinder engine. It required two strong men to swing the engine over"

She was bought by Arthur Kass, who lived beside Connaught Harbour in Portumna. He and his wife, Alma, were Estonian, and had fled the Continent at the end of World War II. His idea was to convert Rambler into accommodation for visiting coarse-fisher-men. She was towed by the ESB tug in about 1967 to Connaught Harbour, where she was completely stripped-out. The hull was divided into double and single cabins, and a large superstructure covered the entire deck—with the exception of the foredeck. She was re-named Calypso.

Unfortunately this venture never got off the ground, due to planning and safety implica-tions. Indeed, Shannon Marine Services (Arthur's company) folded in 1970. Calypso was purchased from the receiver by Ivan Smith who was, at that time, working in South Africa so she lay virtually unused on the north bank below Connaught Harbour. In the mid-1970s, Ivan stripped-out the hull and demolished the superstructure. The Atlantic engine was removed and a six-cyl-inder Ruston air-cooled diesel installed. She reverted to her original name, and a steel deck and wheelhouse were built.

Towards the end of the 1980s Ivan reluc-tantly decided to sell her as pressure of time prevented him from completing the conversion. She was towed up to Shannon Harbour by the Phoenix, to be delivered to her next owner. When she was docked in Shannon Harbour, some plates were found to be cracked and repairs were necessary. Some time later Mick and Fran Stains bought her. At that time the Rambler was partially sunk outside the last lock at Shannon Harbour. They set about re-float-ing her and getting her engine going again. They did a complete refit which had plenty of accommodation.

She was based in Shannon Harbour after that and was used regularly on the Shannon up to around 1998. After that it became a permanent fixture tied up in Shannon Harbour until the current owner John Connon Jnr. bought her. John took her by road back to Ringsend Basin where once again everything was gutted out, including the wheel house as all the decks surrounding it were very badly rusted. He then set about another refit, keeping in mind her age on the outside and comfort on the inside. Five years later most of that work is done and the Rambler is now sitting at Ringsend, awaiting the opening of the Royal Canal to bring her back to her old stomping ground.

Royal Canal Float No. 1
Heritage Boat

Float No. 1 is one of a series of Coras Iompair Eireann (CIE) maintenance craft that were utilised along various designated stretches of the Royal Canal. There were five 'Float' boats in total on the Royal Canal. Unlike the Grand Canal, where the engineering or maintenance craft were usually re-numbered to 'E' (Engineering) barges, on the Royal Canal, the assigned numbers of maintenance came about by use as each 'Float' came onto the system. All the Floats were of different design and not part of any uniform fleet of maintenance craft as they originated from de-commissioned cargo boats that were re-directed to engineering

use. Once a barge became a 'Float', both horses and engines were superfluous to its re-assigned use. At the slow pace of ongoing maintenance and patching, the men attached to each barge would pull the vessel along the short distance to the next stopping point.

The "Float" series of barges were de-commissioned when the Royal Canal closed for navigation in 1961 but most fell into disuse up to a decade or so prior, as the traffic on the system and therefore maintenance works on the Royal declined.

Float No. 1 was sold by CIE, with the relevant paperwork, identifying her as No 1 of the series and a barge of approx 1890 vintage, to a Mr. Boylan in the late 1960's. At that stage she was lying near Binns Bridge, below Drumcondra, on the Dublin end of the Royal Canal. Canal signage visible in the background of an 8mm cine film recording, showing the lift-out, shows what was known as Liffey Junction as being the exact location of the lift. She was originally 70' long but had 10' was cut from her centre portion after she was lifted, to make her compatible in length with the Grand Canal locks. The operation was carried out on a trombone trailer which re-attached the two halves before they were successfully re-welded together. She was subsequently stored near Celbridge / Hazelhatch until a couple of years ago.

Float No.1 is built of iron sheeting, with 2.5" angle ribs, hot riveted, at 2' centres. Her lines include a pointed nose and stern, with a rounded keelson, original design features of a horse drawn barge. She differs from other barges with provenance to the Irish inland waterways system, in that she has a 10' 6" beam, as opposed to the normal 13' on other barges. With an original length of

Float No. 1 was purchased in 2004 by John Dolan and Catriona Hilliard, who are based in Tullamore. They have undertaken a major refurbishment program which includes, hull repairs and future conversion into an engined family barge for ongoing waterways appreciation and use. She will hopefully spend many a happy year on her spiritual home when the Royal Canal navigation is opened fully to the Shannon once again.

70', she could not have navigated either the Ulster Canal or the Grand Canal, due to her being longer than the minimum lock sizes on those navigations. She does have a similar line to the another ex-Royal Canal barge now known as 'The Rambler', although the Rambler is much broader in the beam. Float No. 1 is one of only three Royal Canal barges that are currently in floating condition – the others being "The Rambler" and the Killucan Project Barge.

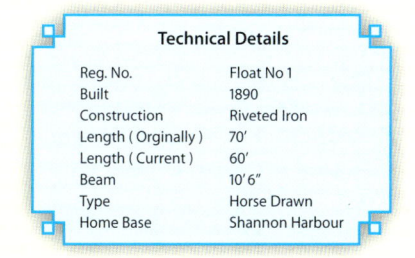

Technical Details	
Reg. No.	Float No 1
Built	1890
Construction	Riveted Iron
Length (Orginally)	70'
Length (Current)	60'
Beam	10' 6"
Type	Horse Drawn
Home Base	Shannon Harbour

Lock keeper at work

Royal Canal Float No. 3
Heritage Boat

T his boat is now known as the Killucan Project Barge and it currently lies opposite Thomastown Harbour on the Royal Canal at the 18th Lock.

Up until 1993 the boat had been lying half full of water a few miles east of Killucan where it lay since the canal was closed by CIE in 1961. The boat's exact origins are unknown but as it measures 60ft x 13ft it was most likely a former GCC Horse Boat. By her design and lines she was built in the late 1900's or early part of the 20th Century and operated as a horse drawn cargo boat. It is not know when she moved to the Royal Canal or whether she worked commercially there before joining the maintenance

"It was one of a series of five maintenance boats referred to as "Floats" used along the Royal Canal"

fleet and being renumbered to Float No. 3. One likely scenario was as horse traffic declined on the Grand she was transferred to the maintenance department and then moved in the early 1950's to the Royal Canal. What is known is that prior to 1961 it was used as a maintenance boat on the Canal. It was one of a series of five maintenance boats referred to as "Floats" used along the Royal Canal. It never had an engine, and was mainly used to carry patching materials (Puddling Clay) to seal the bottom of the canal and rubble to beef up the canal banks. The last crew to work on her were Andrew Flanagan, William Leech and Richard Quinn. Little did they know the boat would be back in action in the area over 40 years later.

In the early 1990's

"It would be used as a floating Museum of Canal Transport with displays of canal flora and fauna. Waterbus trips on the canal and a running commentary of canal sights would give those taking part a flavor of times past"

members of the Royal Canal Amenity Group (RCAG) took on the idea of restoring one of the many derelict barges on the Royal Canal. Having surveyed all the resting hulls on the canal a former maintenance barge lying east of D'Arcy's Bridge in Killucan was selected as giving the best chance of a successful restoration. The boat was available to be bought for £10 from CIE on condition of purchase that when restored it would be used as a floating Museum of Canal Transport with displays of canal flora and fauna. Waterbus trips on the canal and a running commentary of canal sights would give those taking part a flavor of times past.

The proposers of the project ran into problems trying to find a suitable workshop in the greater Dublin area where the restoration could take place and in the end turned to the Executive of the RCAG for support. Eventually, after due consideration, the Killucan Branch of the RCAG agreed to take over the project. Killicuan equally had difficulties in getting a premises but had luck in that Government funding became available to assist in restoring canal boats from the Grand Canal. "Killucan Community and Canal Development Limited" was formed and was successful in securing some of that funding for a barge renovation on the Royal.

Under the terms of the scheme the work was to be carried out as a Community Youth Training Project. The skills to be imparted were metalwork, welding, electrical work, plumbing, and all the skills needed in the complex job of restoring a barge. Trainees would be paid by FAS. A workshop was located at the rear of the Topic newspaper printing works in Mullingar and FAS agreed to pay the rent. The restoration started in January 1996, just as the Celtic Tiger made its debut. The new economic circumstances and the subsequent drop in unemployment made it extremely difficult to find suitable trainees for the project and those that did join left as soon as they had learned the basic skills. With the pool of suitable trainees dwindling the project came to a halt. However by 2000 most of the major fabrication work had been completed, including the replacement of many ribs, the insertion of supports for a floor, a complete replating and the construction of a cabin frame. Waterways Ireland removed the unfinished boat to Thomastown Harbour where it lay on the hard stand for two years.

In the Summer of 2002 members of the community decided that the scheme would die if they didn't take some action. A compressor and sandblasting plant were borrowed from a local businessman. Paint was ordered and within a fortnight the boat was sandblasted and painted.

After some negotiations, Waterways Ireland agreed to assist the completion of the project. A Tullamore based company got the contract to carry out the remainder of the welding and the boat was returned to the water in 2002. Tenders were sent out for the interior refit and by the Summer of 2004 Inhouse Technologies of Dublin had completed the task.

A program of work has been agreed with the Dept. of Marine which, when complete, will allow this restored boat to bring a new lease of life to the restored Royal Canal.

Royal Canal Float No. 15 & 16
Heritage Boats

Two canal boats lie at Darcy's Bridge on the Royal Canal. They look old and damaged, and more than likely incite many a comment from canal walkers not native to the area, or from other visitors who may not know the history of trading boats on that element of the inland waterways system. For those that do, there are many fascinating stories, linked to other tales and families both in and from the surrounding area. One of these who can chronicle the story of these two craft quite well is Mr. Willie Leech.

Willie's dad James was the last trader on the Royal Canal. These two boats are the last remnants of what was once a thriving business. The vessels are known as No. 15 and No. 16. Like the other elements of the inland waterways system, boats on the Royal were numbered. These were horse drawn boats so never had the M (Motor) suffix like those of the Grand Canal and River Barrow

navigations. Both were private boats, No. 15 having been handed down to James Leech from his own father, and James then purchased No. 16 during the war from the Kelly's of Kilcock, another trading family on the Royal Canal.

James Leech was from the Summerhill area of central Dublin, just beside Ballybough Bridge, about a mile from Spencer Dock which is the link of the the Royal Canal to the River Liffey. James built up a substantial fuel business buying coal directly from the coal ships moored just outside Spencer Dock and hauling it back to the midlands. Some of his larger customers included, Maynooth College, Shaws and St. Lomans Hospital in Mullingar. Bagged concrete to Longford and Mullingar along with flour and sugar and of course Guinness were also regular consignments from the city. Cargos into Dublin included turf which was sold by the bag straight from the boat at Ballybough and North Strand area of the city. An unsual cargo was 'mather' a mud similar to what is know as 'puddle' used by the Gas Company in Dublin, to line the lamps and gas grids of the street lighting system. The burnt slag from the mather was recycled, being returned to the midland farmers to use as a kind of fertilizer.

A trip to the city (known as a '3 day trick') needed regular stops to rest the horses, usually two of them for a 50 ton load. The crew would usually comprise 3 men, one at the bow (or at regular intervals down below cooking meals), one on the rudder and a third on the bank with the horse(s). Many of the animals used to pull boats had a previous life pulling either trams or dairy carts in Dublin. They were treated well when working on the boats, with special collars more heavily padded with straw. Fresh grass and the best possible oats from full nosebags at every meal break and of course plenty of fresh water were also the norm. A regular arrangement to rent private stables for them each overnight stop was in place, while the men slept in tight quarters on the craft. When the time came for the horses to retire from the canal, they were usually sold on to local farmers .

As the canal fell into more and more disrepair, the boats needed more regular visits to the dry docks, in both Spencer Dock and Mullingar, to keep them afloat. In the end they were tied up at Darcy's Bridge with the closure of the canal and act as a vivid reminder of the Royals commercial past.

Taking a trip through the lock

Courtesy—Shortall Collection

Chang Sha
Heritage Boat

Chang-Sha was built in 1846, possibly on the Clyde in Scotland, of Lowmore iron plates riveted to iron frames. She was built for one of the directors of the Grand Canal, a gentleman by the name of Sankey as his personal launch, and was known for many years as "Sankey's Steamer". When originally built she was steam powered, and from the dimensions of the propeller opening and the shaft, we can guess that it was a very slow revving engine turning a massive propeller. When we re-plated the bilges in 1989, we found that one of weakest areas was under the current wheelhouse, which apparently coincided with the location of the coal bunkers. The iron having been attacked by the chemicals given off by the coal.

Around the turn of century, she was bought by a Major William Lloyd (Connaught Rangers) of Rockville House, Elfin, who removed the steam engine and boiler and converted her to a house-boat. She was fitted out by Miller and Beatty of Dublin to a very high standard with mahogany panelling. It was Major William Lloyd who gave her the present name and in 1912, he passed the boat on to his son, also a William Lloyd.

There are two explanations for the name Chang Sha. It may refer to the capital city of the Hunan Province because Lloyd holidayed there when he was in China or it or may mean "River House" or "Long Beach" in some Chinese dialect.

Around 1920 she was sold to the Department of Agriculture and was moored in Portumna apparently with the intention of using her as a fisheries research vessel. There is some doubt as to what role she played but it is well known in ecological

Chang Sha at Richmond Harbour c 1929

circles that some of the seminal work on the ecology of the Shannon was conducted by Southern and Gardner in 1922 from a laboratory in Portumna and it seems at least plausible that Chang-Sha played some role in this.

Around 1923 she was bought by Dr Vincent Delaney (father of the founder of IWAI). No engine was fitted to the boat and she was towed to regattas on Lough Ree and Lough Derg for many years by La Vague which the Delaneys also owned or by the Rambler (a Royal Canal boat)

When not in use by the family, the paid hand, who went by the name of "The Pirate" Donnellan, was permitted to live aboard. The family did not use the boat for a number of years and in 1942 she was spotted in a rather sorry state by Syd Shine who asked Dr. Delaney to sell her. When he went aboard to inspect the boat, most of the interior had been gutted to provide wood for the fire and little remained except the marble fireplace.

Syd had her towed to Athlone by the Eclipse Flower and there set about re-fitting her. He initially installed a 2 cylinder Kelvin engine, but this was replaced some time later by a V8 Thornycroft petrol engine with a 100 gallon tank. Syd reckoned he needed 16 gallons of fuel to get to the Lough Ree Yacht Club and back from his berth in Athlone.

Syd used the boat constantly until 1957 when he bought the Fox. He sold her to Alan Dunne in Carrick-on-Shannon for £150 who used her for a number of years. She lay unused in Carrick for several years and was vandalised and eventually sank.

Ken Simmonds bought her some time thereafter, basically to get the gearbox and some other bits and pieces off her and she was again left semi-derelict, this time in

Chang Sha at Carrick—2003

Athlone. In the early 1970s she was bought by Dan Hanovick and Syd towed her to Portlick for him.

No further work was done until she was bought in 1973 by Simon Crowe, who was the drummer with a band called the Boom Town Rats. Simon, built the present super-structure of steel over steel and timber frames and had the Thornycroft engine re-conditioned. Pressure of work forced Simon to sell the boat and she was bought by a consortium of five people, John and David McFarlane, William Prentice, David Browne, and Garry Laird around 1980. They re-fitted the interior again and the Thornycroft engine was removed and replaced by a Perkins S6M.

She was bought by the present owners in February 1988 and they carried out extensive re-plating of the hull that year. A major re-fit of the interior took place in 2002 with an engine upgrade to a Perkins 6354 in 2006

And finally, she may be a canal boat, but Chang-Sha is no barge. She was never used as a trading boat and prefers to be referred to as a Gentleman's Steam Yacht. A lady of leisure for most of her life, she merits inclusion in this book because of her short period with the Dept. of Agriculture!

Coolawn

Heritage Boat

As you pass north of Clashganny Lock you may notice the twisted remains of an old barge on the West bank. This is all that remains of the Steam Boat called the "The Coolawn" which had a colourful history on the Lower Barrow. Oiginally built as a steam boat in Portadown, it was first weighed in 1898. In 1908 she passed ownership from Wallace & McCullagh to a Mr. M.J. Murphy (grandfather of K. Murphy, The Bat) and a Mrs. Prendergast for £127. A new boiler from Ward of Leeds was installed in St. Mullins at this time for £116. Mrs. Prenderdast sold her share to M.J. Murphy in 1913.

The Coolawn was used as a hack boat for his grain and starch business and assisted in the building of Redmond Bridge in Waterford around 1913. At some point it was fitted with a twin cylinder Bolinder engine, which allegedly had a gearbox, a real luxury at the time, in order to manage the tide in the estuary.

The Doherty family ran the boat for many years with canal records showing regular

"legend tells of a trip to Waterford with the Brass Band and the Temperance Society, where on the trip back there were problems with people falling off the Barge because of drink"

journeys in the 40's and 50's, carrying bulk wheat to Waterford, with P. Doherty as Skipper. There were also many journeys listed carrying timber from Bahana Wood

"It then got washed onto the weir at Clohastia at the top of the Ballykeenan lock cut before finally been abandoned above Clashganny lock"

to Waterford and Graignamanagh, though it appears to have been laid up for a year or so in the late forties. When Tim Connolly was laid off work on the canal he was given a job by M.J. Murphy helping to refit The Coolawn after which she transported grain to Waterford for a few years. There are records of nine journeys to Waterford with bulk grain in October – November 1951 alone.

Family legend tells of a trip to Waterford with the Brass Band and the Temperance

Perhaps the start of the trip to Waterford—everyone standing!

on a fore and aft mooring from which it broke free and wedged itself across the bridge, the mark of which can still be seen on the hull today.

The hull was bought from Murphy's and brought up river, with an outboard motor, where it wedged in the locks because it had spread. It then got washed onto the weir at Clohastia at the top of the Ballykeenan lock cut before finally being abandoned above Clashganny lock. After a few years it was moved to the west bank of the river where CIE staff tried unsuccessfully to sink it. She was eventually dragged up on the bank with a bulldozer, the damage to an already wrecked hull is evident today.

Society, where on the trip back there were problems with people falling off the Barge because of drink!

In the mid 50's the boat was finally laid up and left on the quay in Graignamanagh. It was then anchored out on the river

Loading a barge   Courtesy—Shortall Collection

The Fox

Heritage Boat

*P*assing Fox today, snugly secured alongside in Athlone, it's difficult to believe that she is over 140 years old. Yet she was built in 1865, by Grendons of Drogheda, and joined the Grand Canal Company as one of a number of steam tugs, along with the Bat, the Bee and the Fly.

In 1910, she transferred to the Board of Works as the Shannon Navigation maintenance boat, equipped with a Crab Winch crane. In 1923 her steam engine was replaced by a Kelvin four-cylinder petrol/paraffin engine and she was reclassified as a motor barge; the measurement certificate of 12 November 1923 gives 61', 13', 4' 2.25", 42 tons.

L T C Rolt photographed her in the lock at Roosky in 1946. He says in Green and Silver—

Her cheerful skipper lives aboard and leads a roving life repairing locks or re-painting or replacing buoys and markers on nearly 200 miles of river and estuary. The Fox, which carried a crane, was loaded with a miscellaneous collection of gear; baulks of timber, sheer legs, buoys and barrels of tar. She also included a diving suit in her stores.

That diving-suit can be seen in the Waterways Museum in the Grand Canal Docks in Dublin. And years before Rolt met him, Fox's skipper and diver, Dinny Madigan, had made friends in Athlone with a young lad called Syd Shine.

Syd's father was a small farmer near Clonmacnoise. And, as it had been for a thousand and more years, the Shannon was a highway, used amongst other things for carrying turf for sale in Athlone. Syd used the Shannon from an early age; he bought an eighteen foot boat for seven shillings and sixpence, repaired it and sold it for £6, at the age of 14.

"He ran Fox as a training-ship, many of whose cadets are now well-known names on the Shannon"

That money went to pay for Elfin, a 36' sailing boat (to which he added a Model T engine two years later). He and his friends travelled the length of the Shannon, camping on the islands and catching their meals by fishing, shooting and using ferrets. He made his first trip to Dublin along the Grand Canal in 1934; he travelled on the Royal in the same year, when the Grand was closed, bringing an Athlone-built boat to Dublin to be fitted out.

So when Dinny Madigan made friends with the young Syd, he was dealing with someone who, from an early age, had been accumulating experience on the Shannon. And Dinny, who regarded Fox as his own, said to Syd "When I die, won't you look after my boat?"

Time passed. Syd had a successful career, at home and abroad, as musician and

bandleader; he had owned several boats and raced Shannon One-Designs. Kevin Madigan succeeded his father — and then in 1956 the Board of Works laid off the Fox. For a year she lay derelict in the old canal harbour in Limerick, all her gear gone. A child fell in and the family sued the Board of Works, which decided that Fox should be sunk. And at that, Dinny Madigan wrote to Syd and reminded him of his request made all those years ago: "Won't you look after my boat?"

Syd already owned Chang-Sha and didn't really need another 60-footer. But he put in a sealed bid of £30, and then heard that someone else was bidding £40. Syd put in a £50 bid — and found himself the Fox's new owner.

Syd worked on her for six weeks. With the timbers cut in advance, he got the cabin top on in one day. Later on, he extended the wheelhouse and changed the petrol/paraffin engine for a Perkins R6 115hp diesel. The big searchlight on Fox's bow came from David Wheeler, former owner of Schollevaer, who swapped it for a smaller brass one of Syd's. And the Hammond organ had to be cut in two before Syd could

squeeze it in.

It's impossible to capture, in one short article, the full measure of what Syd and Fox have done since then. Syd was a member of the first Council of the IWAI and a frequent participant in rallies, winning prizes and overall awards. He ran Fox as a training-ship, many of whose cadets are now well-known names on the Shannon. He was a regular Shannon One-Design sailor who has been awarded Honorary Life Membership of both the Lough Ree and the Lough Derg Yacht Clubs. He brought the first floating filling-station to Ireland. He participated in an expedition to the first lock on the Ballinamore-Ballyconnell canal back in the 1970s, long before its restoration. He has accumulated an invaluable archive of documents, photographs and mementoes of Fox, of his own activities and of the history of the waterways in this century.

In *By Shannon Shores* (Gill and Macmillan, 1987) Ruth Heard wrote—

Syd [...] has over the years been responsible for introducing many young people to the river, always keeping 'open boat' for those who wanted to join him. Many of these people now have their own boats to bring their families on the river and I am sure they will never forget the debt they owe to Syd.

There's not much one can add to that — except to say that if Dinny is looking down from on high, he'll be pleased at how well Syd Shine, gentleman of the waterways, is continuing to look after his boat.

Jarra

Heritage Boat

The Jarra was previously known as the "Naas" and was built with her sister the "Athy" during 1895 in Chepstow, Gwent, in South Wales. Chepstow is a town on the river Wye which feeds into the Severn and the Bristol Channel. Both boats were designed with a raked hull to increase speed and manoeuverability and were fitted with steam engines. The river and strong tidal conditions of the Severn estuary were very similar to the tidal stretches of the Barrow from the "Scar" (from the Viking word SKAUR, meaning an outcrop of rock) at St. Mullins to the sea. It was here in 1896 that the Naas and Athy commenced working between Waterford and St. Mullins where their owners, the Odlum family, had a flour mill. They brought grain and supplies upriver and returned with sacks of flour. The barges spent the next fifty years in the service of the Odlum family and helped indirectly to feed many a poor family as well.

In 1947 the sisters retired from work. Sadly the "Athy" was sold to Hamilton Lane Foundries in Dublin for scrap metal.

Her sister the "Naas" was purchased by the Grand Canal Company (GCC), towed up the Barrow and scuttled, to help shore up the weir at Milford, five miles below Carlow town. She rested there in a semi submerged state for twenty five years.

In 1972, John McNamara, a CIE engineer, while repairing the nearby lock gate noticed the "Naas" and asked Claude Odlum for the barge. Claude, an ex-Director of the Grand Canal Company, gave John the boat for nothing, on the understanding that John would restore the barge to her former glory. John re-floated the boat and towed her to Tullamore where he worked on her restoration and conversion for the following nine years

In 1981, John had completed his labour of love which more than kept his promise to Claude Odlum. He re-launched the boat and re-named her the "Jara" each letter of the name being the initials of the first names of himself, his wife and their three children (John, Anne, Robert, Ross and Adele). In 1988 John added the wheelhouse which was the last of the major structural work.

John McNamara sold the boat to David Coyle in 1991 and for the following few years David's brother Jasper used it extensively up and down the Shannon. After David's passing away a couple of years ago, John once more got an opportunity to own his labour of love so he bought her back.

In 2006

THE GRAND CANAL, with the system over which the Company trades, serves 3 ports: Dublin, Waterford and Limerick, and 16 counties in the Irish Free State.

CHEAPEST and BEST ROUTE for all kinds of Merchandise to and from Dublin and the undermentioned Stations:—

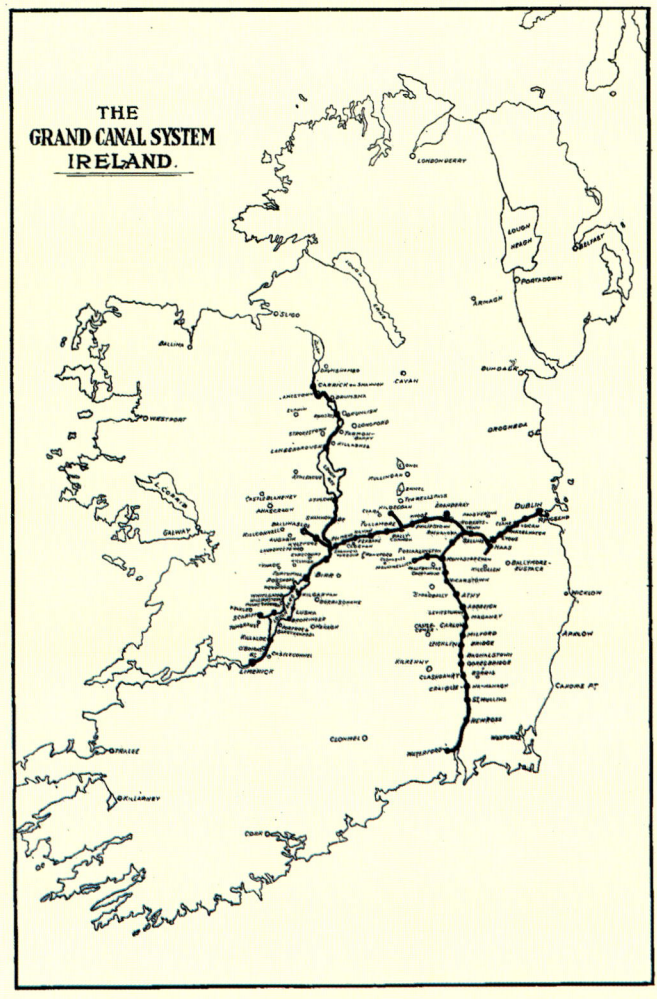

Stations:

- Aylmobn
- Athy
- Bagnalstown
- Ballinasloe
- Banagher
- Belmont
- Carrick-on-Shannon
- Carlow
- Clashganny
- Clondalkin
- Courtwood
- Drominebr
- Edenderry
- Gorebbridge
- Graigue-na-Managh
- Killalor
- Kilbeggan
- Kylemore
- Kilgarvan Quay
- Lanesboro'
- Mountmellick
- Naas
- New Ross
- Prumstown
- Portarlington

Stations:

- Leighlin Bridge
- Levistown
- Limerick
- Luska
- Lyons
- Lucan
- Maganey
- Milford
- Monastervan
- Mountshannon
- Portumna
- Rathangan
- Rahan
- Rhode Bridge
- Robertstown
- Rushey
- Rossmore
- St. Mullins
- Salling
- Scariff
- Shannon Bridge
- Shannon Harbour
- Tullamore
- Vicarstown
- Waterford

Docks at Ringsend, Dublin, to accommodate vessels 148 feet in length.

RATES & OTHER INFORMATION FROM—
H. PHILLIPS, General Manager, James Street Harbour, Dublin.

Tel. Address:
"Granal, Dublin."

Telephones { Dublin 62611 & 62612.
Ringsend Docks, Dublin, 140.

Phoenix
Heritage Boat

The Phoenix was forty years old when the Titanic sank. She was built for Francis Spaight of Derry Castle on Lough Derg, possibly as a wedding present for his son, William. She was based in Killaloe until 1884 and then leased to Arthur Waller, chief brewer in Guinness, who brought her down the Grand Canal — and that must have been fun with her draught!

My great-uncle Harry Lefroy bought her in 1903. Harry and his wife Min (Minchin), used the boat extensively for the next thirty-two years. He owned the Mill in Killaloe, where there was a covered dock, which is one reason for her survival when most other boats of her type rotted away. He used the Phoenix as a floating office and supervised the building of jetties and

up Lough Derg in winter, acting as starting boat for regattas.

Harry re-boilered the Phoenix in 1912: she would do Killaloe Pierhead to Williamstown in one hour flat — which was 12.5mph! In 1927 Harry puchased, for £450, a marvellous two-cylinder, two-stroke diesel engine, made by Ellwe of Sweden. It had a compressed-air start mechanism and developed 36ihp at 475rpm — if it was in good humour.

Harry died in 1935. Min sold Phoenix to a Mr Scott of Scott's Foods in Dublin, who kept her in Howth. He died in 1938 and left the boat to Robert Delamer, his chauffeur, who brought the Phoenix back to Killaloe. Dick Lee of Limerick bought her in February 1940 but worked for the British Admiralty during the war and had little time for his own boat.

After the war, the Phoenix was spruced up and, for the first time, painted white: by tradition, gentlemen's steam yachts were always painted black. "Bunny" Goodbody bought her in 1950, using her from Waterloo Lodge, Kilgarvan, before making the Phoenix his family home in Dromineer for two years.

quays in Portumna, Grange and Spencer's Dock (Lough Allen) amongst others. But her main function was for pleasure: picnics, holiday trips to Lough Allen, shooting trips

She was then laid up in Dromineer for a couple of years before George Newenham, of the Limerick Motor Works, bought her and transformed her. Off came the original teak wheelhouse and the pine main deck. In their place, soft-wood decks, covered in canvas — and a truly appalling wheelhouse made of what looked like tea-chests. George lived on her for a spell, but he was nervous of the engine and never went further than Dromineer. In the late fifties she lay unused, and was home to various people in the Cruising Craft hire-boat company that George's nephew, Hector, had established. In 1962 the Phoenix was re-fitted and did two seasons' hire with a skipper, the late Mick Conroy.

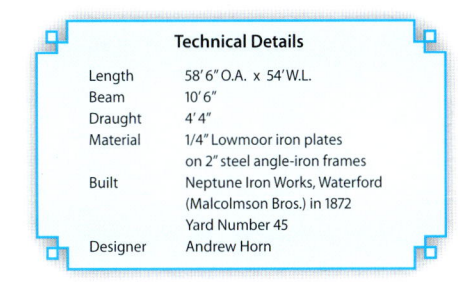

Technical Details	
Length	58' 6" O.A. x 54' W.L.
Beam	10' 6"
Draught	4' 4"
Material	1/4" Lowmoor iron plates on 2" steel angle-iron frames
Built	Neptune Iron Works, Waterford (Malcolmson Bros.) in 1872 Yard Number 45
Designer	Andrew Horn

I borrowed the Phoenix after Christmas 1963 for a trip up the Shannon: ten days of adventure in which the whole family got involved. A deal was struck on 18 January 1964 and we used her as a family boat for a couple of years, finally replacing the old Ellwe engine in 1966 with a Perkins S6. But, as my brother and sister found jobs outside the country and then the gearbox failed, she was little used.

I was now employed with Emerald Star Line and was to move to Portumna. The Phoenix was certainly big enough for Sandra and me to live on, with Delilah the dog; we agreed to buy the boat and she moved to Carrick-on-Shannon for the fitting of new decks, wheelhouse (based on the original design), gearbox and galley. On 9 May 1971 we moved on board: not for the six months we expected, but for eighteen.

During the seventies and eighties, the Phoenix was based in Portumna and used as a tug for grounded hire-boats, a flagship for many sailing events, a commentary vessel for rowing races and, of course, as a houseboat for the family during regattas and for trips up the Shannon. She transported President Childers from Banagher to Clonmacnois

and back to Shannonbridge; she was ready to bring President Hillary from Scarriff to Mountshannon some years later, but for a gale of wind! Much work was carried out— new engine, new aft decks, new fit-out below — to try and bring her back towards her original style.

When we left Portumna, it was back on board until we could find a house in Killaloe. Finally, we built one beside the old canal, with a harbour for the Phoenix at the back door. She is now a venerable 134 years old, and has seen a third century. How much has changed on the river — but again, in a way, how little. When I read the old log, dating from before the first World War, the cadences are all the same — regattas, rain, visitors on board, magic spring days, frostbite trips in winter, picnics in summer — and long may it all continue!

The Bat
Heritage Boat

In the 1850's the Grand Canal Company decided to use steam tugs to speed up the passage times of boats on the canal. For this purpose four boats were built, The Fox, "The Bat", The Fly and The Bee

The original plan was to have the horse boats towed in groups the entire length of the canal but the locks made this too slow so the steam tugs were used on the long levels of the canal.

"The Bat" was built in 1866 in Gorrendons foundry in Drogheda of wrought iron plates on angle iron frames. A steam engine was fitted which took up the rear third of the hull. The steam tugs would have worked on the canal until 1912 when

Killaloe where they lay until 1965. Mick Donahue the lock keeper in Ballycommon bought her for five pounds and subsequently fitted her with accommodation.

Ardnacrusha circa 1927

The Bat towing

the Bolinder engines were introduced. The Bat was fitted with a Bolinder in 1913 and became 25M. She was decommissioned and sold to the ESB in 1927 and used for the construction of Ardnacrusha. After Ardnacrusha "The Bat" was abandoned with Dabu in

He also installed a Gardner 4LW 50-60hp hand-start engine that probably came from an obsolete Bord na Mona bog train at the time. This engine still powers "The Bat".

Mick was famous for scavenging bits and pieces for his barge from anyone and anywhere and these still keep "The Bat" going.

Paul Doran bought "The Bat" from Mick's widow and brought her to Belmont where he fitted an electric start to the engine. He sold it to Noel Dunne who sold it after a short period to Kieran Walsh.

"The Bat" was then on the Shannon Erne Waterway on its opening day and had the privelege of being the first barge into Lough Allen since 1932.

"The Bat" was bought by Ken Murphy & Grainne Duffy in 1999. They have carried out extensive renovations including re-plating her bottom, rebuilding most of the accommodation, electrics and plumbing. A new collapsible wheelhouse was designed and built for passage through Carlow Bridge.

They lived aboard her for a number of years in Graignamanagh before reluctantly moving to a house. "The Bat" cruises the navigation extensively from Graignamanagh to Lough Derg and Ballinamore on the Shannon and down the estuary to New Ross and Inistioge.

Happy Boatmen

Courtesy Shortall Collection

BN.14.

Coill an Eo
Heritage Boat

Coill-an-Eo ("wood of the yew") was built in 1969 in the Liffey Dockyard. She was designed specifically for the Shannon: at 95' x 18' x 4'6" she fits the locks and is shallow enough to cope with low water levels. Coill-an-Eo covers the Shannon as far up as Leitrim and Lough Key, but not Lough Allen or the Shannon-Erne Waterway. She can stand up to serious weather on the big lakes but, with her wheelhouse roof folded down, can also get down to Limerick.

She has a single screw with a 112hp Kelvin engine, but no bow-thruster. A large generator can supply 220v, 110v or three-phase power. The crane in the bow can take various attachments for different jobs.

In the stern is the galley, with the bridge forward of that, above the engine-room. Forward again are two cabins in the hold, each with two pairs of bunks. They are no longer used, as the crew nowadays drive to work.

Coill an Eo in Limerick—2003

Work in progress at Shannonbridge

to be attended to. Some jobs are planned two or three years in advance, but urgent repairs—e.g. when markers go adrift in high winds—may force a change of schedule.

Her first crew were Kevin Madigan (Skipper), Jimmy O'Brien (Fitter) with Michael McMahon and Mick Clifford as deck hands. Bert Conroy joined the crew in 1971 and his son P.J. joined in 1973. Over the years one by one all of that crew became skipper at some stage. P.J. took over from his father in 1992 and was in charge until 2003. George Herriott from Dromineer joined the crew in the late 1980s with Michael. Bert and P. J. George eventually left to take over as skipper of the Fox in the mid nineties. The current crew are John Joe O'Rourke, Tony Burke, Patsy Fallon and Ray McKeown who all joined in the 1990s.

Forward of the cabins is the workshop: Coill-an-Eo and her skilled crew can carry out electrical and mechanical work, including oxy-acetylene cutting and welding, on the spot, wherever she may be. The workshop is roofed with wooden beams and canvas, resting on removable metal cross-pieces, so that the area can be used as a cargo hold if necessary.

Coill-an-Eo carries a "Pioneer Multi", big brother to the near-indestructible dinghies used by many hire-firms, and is usually accompanied by "WB2", a small tug and working platform with a 60hp Lister engine. She is powerful enough to pull Coill-an-Eo off if she has taken the ground while driving markers, but can also get into shallow areas.

The work varies with the seasons. In winter, Coill-an-Eo may be repairing lock gates, towing the pontoon-mounted pile-driving rig or driving the piles to anchor pontoons or as the basis for new or extended harbours. Her experienced crew can drive a 30'–40' section of 18" gun-barrel piling, then weld another section to it in situ, without letting any water in. In summer, even if there is no harbour work in progress, there are navigation marks on the lakes

One unfortunate and sad incident in the Coill-an Eo's history was the tragic loss of a crew member, Tommy Gibbons, in a boating accident in Blackbrink Bay in 1996.

The fleet
WI's Shannon fleet includes the Inspector's launch and RIB, some tugs and the maintenance boat Fox (not to be confused with Syd Shine's Fox), which usually works on the northern reaches. But Coill-an-Eo is the biggest and best-equipped, and an essential element in the maintenance and improvement of the Shannon Navigation.

ESB Nº. 1 & ESB Nº. 2
Heritage Boats

Both Boats were built in Germany by Ziegret Boizenbarg in 1924. They were purchased new and brought to Ireland by the Siemens Company when they were contracted by the Irish Government to build the Hydro Station at Ardnacrusha.

These two boats are unique in that they were the only steel boats to work on the Irish waterways that had timber bottoms. After the building of Ardnacrusha in 1932, both boats were purchased by the ESB from Siemens for the price of £200 pounds each.

They were both used by the ESB Maintenance Department as dumb boats (without engines) and were towed around by an ESB Tugboat to various projects. Type of projects included carrying materials up and down the headrace on grouting operations, drilling operations and concrete plating maintenance. Both were involved in the salvage of 62M in 1953. She had sunk with a load of cement while being towed by the St. Patrick two years previously. ESB engineering drawings for the salvage operation make interesting reading.

ESB No. 1 Serial Number 13566

The ESB Civil Works Plant Spec. Sheet from 1932 indicates she is 18.03M in length with a width of 4.22M and a height of 1.4M. She has 6mm steel sides with a flat bottom constructed of timber and had a capacity of 51 tonnes.

Unlike her sister ship, ESB No.1 had her cargo hold covered over with timber to make a solid working platform. When purchased by Gerry Burke in 1991 she was lying on the canal outside the ESB depot in Killaloe with her wooden floor leaking. Her hull was being pumped out every couple of weeks. Gerry planned to tow her up to Lough Derg with 68M but on Sunday April 8th when we went to move her a flood on the river resulted in a huge torrent of water coming down the canal. 68M towing another boat didn't have enough momentum to get through the restriction of the

ESB No. 2 Working

disused lock on the canal so Joe Treacy's (4E) assistance was called upon and progress was made through with the aid of a tow from Joe's jeep. She is currently lying partly submerged and sitting in the soft mud of Church Bay awaiting a long deserved makeover and a new bottom.

ESB No. 2 Serial Number 13556
The ESB Civil Works Plant Spec. Sheet from 1932 says she is 18.04M in length with a width of 4.2M and a height of 1.4M. She has 6mm steel sides with a flat bottom constructed of timber and had a capacity of 53 tonnes.

ESB No. 1—2006

ESB No.2 was craned out at the pier head in Killaloe in the early 90's as her timber bottom needed to be replaced. The work wasn't done and she lay upside down at the pier head until purchased by Gerry Burke in 2001. By then the timber bottom had all but disappeared but the oak ribs across the bottom were in good shape. He took advantage of her lying upside down and got Patrick Minogue to weld on a new steel bottom before she was craned back into the river. On May 1st 2002 there was a few anxious moments getting the William O'Brien Crane into the site to lift and turn the barge. While turning the barge it slipped from the crane and damaged a boundary fence. While crane hire is always a big expense in these situations, in this case the subsequent fixing of the fence cost a lot more. Once in the water she was towed by 68M to Church Bay to join her sister.

In September 2004, for Water Heritage day, the Burke gang took ESB No. 2 to Dromineer with 68M to collect 1,000 bales of barley straw which they brought across the lake to Dromaan. ESB No. 2 is now patiently awaiting a spurt of energy from her owner to start its conversion, which is due any day soon.

ESB No. 2—2006

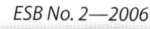

St. Ciaran & St. Brendan
Heritage Boats

The St. Ciaran , who's original name was "Wroxham Belle", was built at Rowhedge near Colchester in 1936 by Rowhedge Ironworks. She was the first motor-driven passenger boat on the Norfolk Broads. At the outbreak of the war she was commandeered for patrol work on the Broads (RN) before been shipped out to Sierra Leone as deck cargo. She later returned and went back to work on the Thames at Teddington.

The St Brendan was originally named "Cardinal Wolsey", She travelled from England to the Shannon under her own power in 1957.

In 1954 a group of VIP's were brought for a trip on the Shannon aboard the St. Clare and they became convinced of the rivers potential. In 1956 CIE was charged by the government to develop boating on the Shannon. CIE sourced and acquired two boats in England, one of which was the "Wroxham Belle" which was re named "St

Ciaran". The other "Cardinal Wolsey" was renamed the "St. Brendan".

The boats required minimum headroom of 14' and that was enough to ensure that no low fixed bridges would be built across the Shannon.

The St. Ciaran was mostly stationed at the old railway terminus at Ballina (Killaloe), giving short cruises in that area. She occasionally ran from other points along the Shannon such as Portumna and Banagher.

The St. Brendan was stationed in Athlone and ran cruises around Lough Ree up as far as Lanesborough.

CIE installed new Thornycroft RNR 6MV engines in each boat, along with maple decks and canopies for dancing, public address systems and coloured lights run off a generator. The boats were used intensively for many years catering for day tours, school trips, etc. giving many people their

St. Ciaran

St. Brendan

first trip on the river. CIE ran day tours from Dublin, transporting people to the cruises and back again.

In 1974 both boats were offered for sale by tender and Dick Fletcher who was running a cruising restaurant business in New Ross was successful in buying the St. Ciaran. He subsequently managed to buy the St. Brendan in 1977 . Dick made substantial changes to both vessels, putting the helms aft, adding extra seating, raising decks and enabling easier access to saloons, galley accommodation and toilets. The windows have been enlarged on both boats. He installed a Gardner six cylinder engine which gives little vibration and low noise at only 1500 rev. Both have been involved in the Galley business since 1974 bringing passengers on cruises up the Nore, Suir and the Barrow. The business is now running under the ownership of the Minihan family. While the St. Ciaran is still in operation with lunch, afternoon tea and dinner cruises the St. Brendan is currently lying idle.

Guinness Liffey Barges
Heritage Boats

*O*ne cannot write a book on Inland Waterway Barges without reference to the Guinness Barges that plied their cargo on the one mile run from St. James's Street Quay to the Custom House docks. The steam driven barges conjure up romantic memories for Dubliners as they remember the smoke filled stacks being lowered to go under O'Connell Bridge at high tide.

The Guinness Barges were truly a part of Dublin, being a daily sight since the opening of the first jetty at St. James's Quay in 1873. Sadly the development of road transport tankers, the building of new ships with massive stainless steel tanks, the advancement of brewing techniques, and the building of breweries elsewhere, marked the death knell for the Guinness Liffey Barges which finally ceased to sail on midsummer day 1961.

The original Guinness jetty built in 1873 consisted of three berths – 1st, 2nd & 3rd.

An additional berth was added in 1887 known as 1st Empty, another in 1890 known as Shannon's Berth and finally a last one built in 1892 known as 2nd Empty. The jetties were extended in 1913 with a further 5 added, 3 empty and 2 loading. These developments followed closely the growth of the Guinness export trade during this period.

The first fleet of Guinness barges were numbered up to No. 9, but little is known of them other than No. 9 was bought by the Grand Canal Company and used as a tug on the Shannon in 1916. The barges that are best remembered were in fact two separate fleets which were named after Irish Rivers, and later after Dublin place names. Many a Dubliner took pride in been able to name all of the Guinness barges!

The first Guinness river fleet— River names.

The first fleet of river class barges started with the *Lagan* which was built by Harland & Wolfe in Belfast in 1877. Six later in 1883 Guinness took delivery of the *Shannon,* a barge which had a rudder and propeller at each end. The next 10 barges were of a more conventional design and were delivered as follows—*Liffey* 1888, *Lee* 1889, *Boyne* 1891, *Slaney* 1892, *Suir* 1892, *Foyle* 1892, *Moy* 1897, *Vantry* 1902, *Dodder* 1911 and the *Tolka* in 1913. The *Docena* was purchased second hand in England in 1920.

No.10—The Lagan, 1877, Harland & Wolfe, Belfast

The first of the steam driven barges, No. 10 called *Lagan* was steam powered by a marine return tube type boiler with a deliver pressure of 100lbs. The boiler, measuring 6ft diameter and 6ft long, drove a two cylinder reciprocating engine that powered the twin screws. Another smaller engine of the same type was fitted amidships to drive the crane which could lift 12½ hundredweights (635 kg).

No.11—The Shannon, 1883, Messrs. Allsop, Preston

No.11—The *Shannon* was a different type of barge. She was steam powered and twin screw, but the propellers and rudder were fitted at each end i.e. fore and aft. She was a lot longer than No.10 and could not swing around at the jetty, but could go up and down the river without having to turn around. She had a more powerful engine than No.10 as she had long drive shafts from the engine room which was amidships. The loco type boiler fitted crosswise across the driving shaft, i.e. port to starboard, giving 100lbs pressure. The engine room of this barge was very hot and very uncomfortable for the drivers, as when she was under way as she had the main engine, the crane pillar, the crane engine fitted horizontally to the roof and the driving shaft all fitted in the centre. The driver had to come up the ladder from the port side on to the deck and go down another on the starboard side to keep on minding his boiler and oiling his engine and looking after his pumps.

No.11 had a berth all to herself at the jetty known as the Shannon's berth which had three hand winches fitted for unloading. Her regular cargo was 110 butts for Holyhead and Birmingham stores.

No.12—The Liffey, 1888, Ross & Walpole, Dublin

Built in Dublin by Ross and Walpole she was the same type as the No.10 but a bit larger. She was originally given the name *Anna Liffey* but as this was already in use by another boat it had to be changed to *Liffey*. She was the first of the new barges to be built in Dublin. Her load was 230 hogsheads or 110 butts and 16 hogsheads.

An interesting detail to No.12 and No.14 is that they were both commandeered by the British Government during the 1914-18 war and that No.14 saw some service on the canals in France.

No.13—The Lee, No.14—The Boyne, No. 15—The Slaney, No. 16—The Suir, No. 17—The Foyle, No. 18—The Moy and No.19—The Vantry

Nos. 13–19 were all built to the same size and specification as the No.12. Following each other between 1889 and 1902.

Hull Size	80' x 17.1' (82' x 19' with belting).
Hull	Clinker built 3/8" Keel Plate, 5/16" bottom plate and ¼" plate
Gross Tons	81.19 Tons.
Net Tons	47.12 Tons.
Boiler	Return Tube 7' by 7'6" Long. One furnace, working pressure 160 lbs / inch.
	Built by A. Anderson & Sons, Glasgow.
Engine	BHP 135 at 165 rpm.
	Built by Messrs. McKie & Baxter, Glasgow.
Crane	Steam Driven, load 12 ½ cwt at 100lbs/inch.
	Built by Messrs. Clarke Chapman.
Propeller	Cast Iron. Four Blade 4'11" diameter by 7' Pitch.
Speed	Full load (105 1/2 tons) = 7 ½ knots.
Capacity	Two coal bunkers @ 1 ½ tons = 3 Tons.
	Two fresh water tanks@568 galls each = 5.07 Tons.
	One forepeak tank 2131 galls. = 9.5 tons.
	Hold size 4,450 cubic feet under deck level.
Draft	6' with when fully loaded.
Steering	Donkin's Screw gear with shaft and bevel wheels
Lamps	One port & one starboard, one mast head, one stern.
Painting	Entire hull inside to have three coats and outside two coats of best red lead
	paint, each coat to be well dried before next is put on. The bottom and topsides
	to have a final coating in Messrs A. Guinness & Co. approved colours.

Guinness Barges were built to Lloyds Classification A1 for River Traffic.

No. 20—The Dodder, 1911, Ross & Walpole, Dublin

Built in 1911 she was the same size as the other barges but had no mechanical power or winch and therefore relied on other barges to be towed and discharged. She could carry a larger load of 260 hogsheads or 130 butts.

A petrol driven crane similar to that on the "Tolka" was fitted later.

No. 21—The Tolka, 1913, Ross & Walpole, Dublin

This barge was known as the *motor boat* as she had two Brooks Marine petrol engines of 55hp each which were mounted on deck. The engines were geared down below deck to twin reciprocal screws. A petrol driven crane (Brooks Marine 35Hp) was mounted amidships that worked faster and better than the steam cranes. Because of the introduction of petrol engines the drivers were supplied from the Guinness garage, until the Engineering Department took

over in 1921. As these engines were cranked by hand, starting them tested the might of any man at 4am on a frosty morning.

No 22 - The Docena

The Docena was bought second-hand in England in 1920 and towed over. She was slightly smaller than the existing barges with different hold and equipment layout. Her triple expansion steam engine with condenser drove a single screw. The boiler was a tube type, 5'6" diameter which was smaller than the 6'6" boilers fitted on the other barges. Her funnel was larger than her counterparts but balanced by a large weight to ease the lowering at bridges. One long hold was serviced with a small winch and high mast (45') with a derrick, mounted on the forward deck which could reach any part of the hold to discharge cargo. She could carry up to 200 hogsheads and had seen her best days before coming to Guinness.

The Second Guinness Fleet— Dublin Place Names.

This new fleet consisted of ten 80′ motor barges and which were built by Vickers (Ireland) Ltd., (Dublin Dockyard Company) and made its debut on the 29th November 1927 with the arrival of the first barge *Farmleigh*. The remaining 9 barges *Knockmaroon, Chapelizod, Fairyhouse, Castleknock, Clonsilla, Killiney, Sandyford, Howth* and *Seapoint* were delivered in succession up to 1931. They were of similar specification and fit out, being 80′ long by 17′ beam with a draft of over 6′ when fully loaded and a very different barge from

"we did sail down the river and they were sniping at one another across the Liffey. I need not tell you that the only man on deck was the skipper"

those of the previous fleet. Being well equipped and easy to manoeuvre they were ideally suited for the type of work required and could deliver 7½ knots with a full load of 105 tons.

1920-22

There are various accounts in the Guinness archives of extraordinary behaviour of the Guinness crews during the period of the War of Independence and the subsequent Civil War. During the Black and Tan period when Dublin was under curfew all drivers and boatmen were issued a pass from Dublin Castle so they could start

"during the whole of the Second World War not one cross channel boat of our own or belonging to any of our other companies left the port of Dublin one minute late due to any delay from the barges"

work at the jetty in the early mornings in order to deliver their precious cargo on the tide to the steam ships at the Custom Quay. It was only coincidental that most of this cargo was due for consignment to England.

There were other times during this troubled period when passage through the city was considered unsafe and the drivers and boatmen slept in the Brewery premises while continuing to maintain their daily delivery schedule.

Later in 1922 there are accounts of the barges continuing to operate along the Liffey as the Civil War started with the assault of

NB: Larger image on page 109

the Four Courts by the Free State Army and gunfire continued to be exchanged across the river for about a week.

To quote an extract from John Doyle Foreman i/c Boat Engine Drivers... *"Anyway, we did sail down the river and they were sniping at one another across the Liffey. I need not tell you that the only man on deck was the skipper. There was a lot of firing going on in O'Connell Street too. We sailed all during that week and got an extras week's pay as danger money. There was not a day at that time but at least eight barges sailed fully loaded from the jetty to Dublin Port,"* despite the troubles at that time.

Later during the Emergency 1939–1945 when fuel was scarce, Doyle highlighted that it was... *"The proud boast of the boat engine drivers was that during the whole of the Second World War not one cross channel boat of our own or belonging to any of our other companies left the port of Dublin one minute late due to any delay from the barges."*

The above extract highlights the dedication and commitment to duty that was characteristic of the Guinness drivers and crew.

Work done by Crews

While the Guinness barges were well equipped with cranes etc., there should be no underestimation of amount of work involved in loading & unloading the Barges

daily. It was not unusual for the two men in the hold, and jetty and bogie gang of 8, to load 1000 casks a day and up to 1500 in 12 hours. The cross channel steam Ships would carry about 1600 casks which could take up to 12 hours to discharge and load. Hence the attractiveness of having your own crane aboard.

Mishaps

Working on the Guinness barges was not without incident and there are numerous records showing the detailed investigation of mishaps along with methodical efficiency with which they were resolved. It was not unusual for a barge to sink due to a combination of adverse weather with a full load or collision. What is remarkable was the speed in which these larger barges would be recovered, boilers overhauled, hull inspected and painted and re-launched sometimes within a matter of days.

Other reports deal with "contact" incidents between boats in what was a busy traffic channel on the Liffey, and the consequential 3rd party settlements. Again the reports are brief, to the point, outlying the facts and remedy. No time wasting here!

There is an account of the sinking of No.22, the *Docena*. A very strong easterly gale was blowing as the barges sailed down the river in late 1927. As the barges had no deck combing, a number of them started to take a lot of water into the hold. The immediate action for such an event was to make for the nearest quay and discharge some of the cargo, raising the freeboard and recover the load later. Unfortunately, the *Docena* was the last barge coming down the river and on coming through Butt Bridge took a lot of water on very fast. She headed at speed for the Custom House Quay. The driver had only managed to get the mast and derrick up (to discharge the cargo) with her bow on the quay when she went down. The crew got ashore safely with only the

clothes they were wearing. The recovery of the barge was contracted out to the Port & Docks who had her lifted and towed to slip within two days, and handed back ready for work within 19 days.

The demise of the Guinness Liffey Barges

The early 30's were an intensely busy period for the Liffey barges, right up until 1937 when the building of the Guinness Brewery in Park Royal (London) reduced the export demand from Dublin and took a lot of the port work from the fleet. Shortly after this, in mid 1938, the *Farmleigh* and *Fairyhouse* were sold off. *Farmleigh* went to the Royal Navy in Scapa flow under her own steam and the *Fairyhouse* steamed to the mouth of the Humber via Caledonian Canal. She later served with distinction in the evacuation from Dunkirk. The *Knockmaroon* and *Chapelizod* were sold in late 1938. The end of the emergency of 1939-1945 saw the return of plentiful supplies of fuel for the new fleet of Guinness trucks which took over from the barges and over a period of a few years. The fleet was gradually decommissioned and sold off. Six of the barges were acquired by Scots of Toomebridge, for addition to their fleet of sand barges on Lough Neagh. They were *Foyle*, *Lagan*,

Killiney, *Chapelizod*, *Castleknock* and the *Clonsilla* which were all sailed up the East coast to the north coast of Co. Antrim and towed up the River Bann to Lough Neagh. Here their holds were altered to accommodate their new role as sand barges. Over the years they were re-engined several times and eventually finishing up with six cylinder Gardiner diesel power units that could deliver up to seven knots under load. The *Foyle* was later sold to Hutchinson Ltd on Lough Neagh and saw out her days there.

Where are they now?

Of the twenty-two boats in the combined fleets, no fewer than nine ended their days on Lough Neagh, where they were used in the sand trade. The *Vartry* lies half sunk west of the breakwater at the entrance to the floodgates at Toomebridge. The *Slaney* lies in the Queens Gap on the Lower Bann north of Toome Canal. The *Boyne* forms part of the harbour wall at P. J. Wall's quay in Toome Bay. The *Chapelizod* and the *Castleknock* were lost by explosion during the 1970's, although parts of them can be seen at Scotts Hutchinson's site. The *Clonsilla* foundered in a storm in Toome Bay (the skipper was rescued by a Lough Neagh fishing boat) and lies in seventy feet of water off Doss. The *Foyle* is half buried in the sand at the mouth of the Crumlin River in Lennymore Bay. The *Lagan* forms part of the Quay at Scotts Sandy Bay site. The *Killiney* is lying off Ballyginnif as part of the breakwater.

Tim Magennis says that the *Shannon* was wrecked off Balbriggan while the *Suir* went to work on the River Slaney and the *Moy* to the River Suir. And there are three *Farmleigh*-class boats near Waterford. Two are sunk in the mouth of the Kilkenny Blackwater, which flows in to the Suir just above Waterford; the third is still afloat at Fastnet Shipping, whose principal Martin O'Hanlon used her, when he was much younger, to dredge for sand up the Suir, operating the vessel single-handed. Her engine-room has been shortened and she now has a wheelhouse and a funnel that would never have fitted under the Liffey bridges, but the original worm steering is still to be seen. Unfortunately inspection has failed to find the names of any of these three *Farmleigh*-class boats, but Martin O'Hanlon's may be the last Guinness Liffey Barge still afloat.

Lough Neagh Sand Barges
Heritage Boats

The largest commercial enterprise working on Lough Neagh, which is also the most significant commercial inland waterways activity on this island, is the sand extraction business. Thousands of tons of sand are dredged daily from the bottom of the Lough to feed the booming construction industry. The sand is also used in a range of products from roof tiles to massive concrete bridge sections. Over seven thousand tons was delivered to Croke Park as a base for the playing surface.

Nine of the twenty-two Guinness Liffey Barges ended up their service as sand barges on Lough Neagh. In addition there were at least two M Boats (44M & 64M) that found their way to Lough Neagh after the cessation of trade on the Grand Canal. They both had their Bolinder engines removed and were used as dumb barges, towed by a Bantam tug.

At least six of the John Kelly dumb barges, used on the Lagan for hauling imported coal from the John Kelly coal boats, were used in the sand trade. Some were used with tugs, and others were redesigned and fitted with diesel engines. Quite a few barges were manufactured locally in Portadown Foundry and one, the *Kathleen*, which was last used as a pump boat in Toome Bay, can be seen at Milltown at the Head of Benburb Gorge on the Ulster Canal.

At present there are sixteen barges working on Lough Neagh with carrying capacity ranging from two hundred to five hundred tonnes. All are loaded by pump, which brings a slurry of sand and water aboard into a settlement tank, with the excess water running overboard back into the Lough.

There are three methods used for discharging the load ashore: grab crane (the simplest); discharge by hopper into the harbour and pumped ashore; or adding

Copyright, GUINNESS Archive, Diageo, Ireland

water to the settlement tank and pumping ashore as a slurry (the most common method). A method no longer used was to have a pump boat anchored offshore and pump the sand ashore by pipeline. Another method no longer used was to have a

Scotts have the largest and only purpose-built fleet: six identical barges, 120′ 6″ by 19′ 3″ and all loaded and discharged by pump. They were built Bann-max (the largest size for the locks on the Lower Bann) by James W. Cook Ltd. of Wivenhoe, Essex. These are the *William James* (the earliest: built 1968), *Ram's Island*, *Coney Island* (the latest: 1974), *Sandy Bay*, *Ballyronan* and *Toomebridge*. Two other barges of this class, the *Lough Neagh* and the *Ballyginnif*, were lost by explosion during the 1970's. Sadly three lives were lost during this incident.

barge with a grab anchored offshore to load other barges which came alongside.

The majority of the barges working on Lough Neagh today are Dutch barges bought secondhand on the Continent. Some have been sailed across the North Sea and the Irish Sea and up the Lower Bann while some—at 200 feet long with a beam of 30 feet, being too big for the Lower Bann—have been brought in by road. One, the *Tramp*, was delivered in two halves and welded back together at Antrim. The Emersons sand-barge dredgers the 500-tonne 170ft *Norman* and the *Nijverheid* (renamed the *Bay Shore*) were delivered by road and launched at Toome Bay.

Today's fleet consists of the *Norman* (Emersons), the *Bay Shore* (Emersons), the *Tramp* (Lagans), the *Fairhead* (Lagans), the *Libertas* (Mulhollands), the *Lennie* (Mulhollands), the *Delcapo* (Walls), the *Sandpiper* (RMC), the *Tredagh* (RMC), the *Gylfe* (RMC) plus the six barges belonging to Scotts of Toomebridge listed below.

Acknowledgements
Sources & Bibliography

Primary Sources
Grand Canal Weight Ledger, Killaloe. – Courtesy of Robert Bayly
D'Arcy, Gerard - *Portrait of the Grand Canal*, Transport Research Associates, 1969.
Delaney, Ruth - *By Shannon Shores*, Gill & Macmillan 1987.
Canalianna, Robertstown, Muintir na Tire, 1965-80.
Delaney, Ruth - *The Grand Canal of Ireland*, David & Charles 1973.
Delaney V.T.H. and D.R. - *The canals of the south of Ireland*, David & Charles 1966.
Rolt, L.T.C. - *Green & Silver*, Allen & Unwin, 1949.
The Grand Canal, Inchicore & Kilmainham, 1991
Shorthall Robert, Photographic Collection.
Contributions made from individual barge owners.
The Canalmen's Association - Detailed discussions with former canal men.
(Description of crew details and crew changes are as related verbatim by former canal men)

CIE Papers / Documents
Payroll Ledger for the closing of the Grand Canal, Carlow and Main Branch 1/1/60
Canal Boat Listing – 1980's

Guinness Archive, Guinness Storehouse, St. James's Gate Dublin 8
Canal & River Navigation, Edward W. Paget Tomlinson
The Guinness Harp - Jan/Feb 1961- J Doyle
Specifications – River Barges 1928
Memo's - Ross & Walpole 1912
Memo's – Port & Docks Office, Dublin 1910
Memo's – Lloyds Register of Surveys
Guinness Internal Memos – Engineer in Chief & Managing Director1905
Guinness Transport Office - Board Endorsements No. 427
Guinness Photographs – Guinness Liffey Barges & St. James Street Harbour

Other Sources.
IWAI News - Lough Neigh Sand Barges, Michael Savage
IWAI News – The Guinness Liffey barges, Michael Savage / BJ Goggin
IWAI News – M Barges & Bolinders – Oliver Connolly
Inis na Mara – Where are the barges now? - Tim Magennis

The Heritage Boat Association would like to acknowledge the generous help and assistance that was forthcoming from all those that were associated with the research and publication of this book.

Robert Shortall
Photographer (1918-1981)

Robert (Bob) Shortall was born in New Ross, Co. Wexford in 1918. From an early age he was inquisitive of all that was happening around him. He got into photography at the early age of 14 when he got his first camera, a Brownie box camera. From then, he set out to record in photographs what he saw going on around him. In the late 1940's he progressed to a Leica camera which, at the time, was the Rolls-Royce of cameras.

Film was his second passion and for twenty four years he worked as a projectionist at the Coliseum Cinema in Waterford. Throughout his life Bob recorded in both

photo and film the last of the Sailing Schooners, Canal boats (barges) and Steam Trains and while he sadly passed away in 1981, he has left behind him a wonderful legacy.

The Heritage Boat Association is privileged to have permission from his brother Paddy to reproduce some of these images in this book.

The Young Robert Shortall (on left)

Robert Shortall